ICY WINTERS
ON THE
CHESAPEAKE
BAY

ICY WINTERS
ON THE
CHESAPEAKE
BAY

A HISTORY

JAMES L. FOSTER

THE
History
PRESS

Published by The History Press
Charleston, SC
www.historypress.com

First published 2021

Manufactured in the United States

ISBN 9781467148696

Library of Congress Control Number: 2021945857

CONTENTS

Contents

CONTENTS

CONTENTS

PREFACE

W hen it comes to climate, it seems that we are predisposed to recall extreme seasons and years more vividly than ones that may have been bountiful but otherwise not particularly newsworthy. I suppose this is especially true if a remarkably snowy or cold winter occurs during one's formative years—before reaching adulthood. Though I was a decade past my teenage years in 1977, the winter of 1976–77 left an indelible impression on me. Living in the Washington, D.C. suburbs, deprived for seven or eight years of a decent snowstorm, I was hoping to experience a winter that mattered. If a big snowstorm was not in the equation (and it was not in 1977), then an icy cold winter would have to suffice. The snow may have refused to pile up, but that winter the ice piled up in memorable heaps on the Chesapeake Bay. Not since the winter of 1917–18 had the bay's waters been so chilled. As I write this, forty-four years after the epic winter of 1976–77, it is natural to wonder if another such offering will plaster the bay with ice. It may be that great, icy winters on the Chesapeake Bay are like great comets—their return periods are measured in decades, if not centuries. But at least with comets, their returns can be predicted.

I would like to acknowledge all the wonderful historical societies in the counties surrounding the Chesapeake Bay. In particular, I'd like to recognize, in Maryland, the Cecil County Historical Society, the Talbot County Historical Society (Peggy Morey), the Anne Arundel County Historical Society, the Baltimore County Historical Society, the Calvert County Historical Society, the Dorchester County Historical Society, the Harford

County Historical Society, the Howard County Historical Society and the Montgomery County Historical Society.

Robert J. Hurry of the Calvert Maine Museum (visit this museum if you haven't already) was instrumental in guiding me to valuable resources and photographs. The Chesapeake Bay Maritime Museum (St. Michaels) and the Maryland Historical Society (Baltimore) are treasure troves for researchers looking for anything related to the Chesapeake Bay and maritime Maryland history. Also, John Gallagher of the Maryland Department of Natural Resources was very giving with his time. The Zane Brothers Company and Blaise Willig were especially generous in allowing me to use their photographs.

I'm grateful to the Associated Press News (Mathew Lutts), the *Baltimore Sun* newspapers (Tim Thomas) and the *Virginia-Pilot* newspapers (Tony Dudek) for directing me to their impressive archives.

Furthermore, I'd like to thank Dr. Dorothy Hall and Dr. Darrel Williams for the MODIS images and for the Landsat images, respectively. Thanks, too, to Jeff Masek and Mike Taylor for enhancing the February 1, 1977 Landsat image of the Chesapeake Bay. Dorothy also helped improve the quality of several of the images that appear in this book. I'd also like to thank Dr. Joey Comiso and Dr. Peter Wasilewski, who provided useful insights regarding the formation of ice in salty and brackish waters.

My former next-door neighbor and longtime friend Howard Rush and I occasionally hiked to nearby Northwest Branch when we were kids to "skate" across its frozen, hard surface. Later, Bob Leffler and I visited the shores of the iced-over Chesapeake Bay during the that phenomenal winter of 1977, and the following year (in early March), we walked across a portion of the frozen Tridelphia Reservoir—two unforgettable winters. Thanks to both of you gents for lasting memories that inspired me to learn more about our "backyard" bay.

I'm, of course, very thankful for my family (Pat, Jack, Shane, Cindy and Chen) and for my friends and colleagues who offered encouragement, helpful comments and suggestions.

A special thanks is due to Kate Jenkins (acquisitions editor) and Ashley Hill (copy editor) for their help and patience with me in guiding this project to fruition. My gratitude is also expressed to Debbie Keller, Linda Hill and the "Confabulators" for their support and constructive observations.

Finally, I want to acknowledge longtime watermen Robbie Wilson and Russell Dize for their wise observations and lively conversations.

1
GEOGRAPHY OF THE CHESAPEAKE BAY

The Chesapeake Bay is the prized gem of the many jewels making up the waterways of the mid-Atlantic coast of the United States. The Chesapeake's tidal shoreline (at high tide) stretches approximately 7,325 miles; adding in the mileage of its tidal tributaries, this total increases to 11,684 miles. Still, there are few places along its main shoreline where this water-filled gouge is so wide that the far shore cannot be glimpsed.

The bay takes in water from an area totaling nearly sixty-four thousand square miles—from most all of Maryland, about half of Virginia, Delaware and Pennsylvania and about one-fifth of West Virginia and New York.[1] Captain John Smith said of the bay: "Heaven and earth never agreed better to frame a place for man's habitation…with fruitful and delightsome land."[2]

On a journey from Cape Henry, north to the Susquehanna Flats, a helmsman need not vary his or her course by more than two compass points from due north. Sailing the length of the bay, you cruise past 48 noteworthy rivers, as well as 102 streams, but you quickly lose count of all the springs and sloughs that drain into the bay.[3]

William Robertson said it is the "noblest bay in the universe…that grand reservoir into which are poured all the vast rivers.…[They] open the interior parts of the country to navigation and render a commercial intercourse more commodious than in any other region of the globe."[4] According to its earliest European visitors, the Chesapeake Bay deserved such a highly colored description.

A majority of the bay's water volume, between 50 and 55 percent, flows south from the Susquehanna River; another 20 to 25 percent is contributed by the southeastwardly drain of the Potomac River. However, aside from the Susquehanna and Potomac Rivers, none of the other rivers entering the Chesapeake Bay could be called "vast." It should be pointed out that the bay receives nearly half of its input from the Atlantic Ocean (salt water).

The Chesapeake Bay and the Susquehanna River (the sixteenth-largest river in the United States in terms of drainage area) emerged from beneath the melting glaciers of the last ice age, some ten thousand years ago.[5] In fact, the Chesapeake Bay formed when the Susquehanna River was flooded by torrents of meltwater draining from ice as much as a mile thick in what is now northern Pennsylvania and southern New York. Because the Susquehanna River's original natural channel extends to where the bay enters the Atlantic Ocean, deep-water shipping is possible to ports as far up the bay as Baltimore and to the Chesapeake and Delaware Canal, despite the Chesapeake being

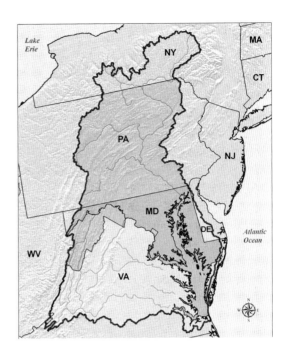

Opposite: A Landsat 8 composite image of the Chesapeake Bay as observed in October and November 2014. *Courtesy of the USGS Earth Resources Observation and Science (EROS) Center.*

Right: A map showing the drainage area of the Chesapeake Bay. *Courtesy of the USGS Department of Agriculture, Natural Resources Conversation Service.*

a shallow embayment (as all estuaries are). It is thought that the present configuration of the river and bay did not appear until approximately three thousand years ago.[6]

The bay extends across nearly three degrees of latitude, from 36.9 to 39.6 degrees north, from the Susquehanna Flats to the Virginia Flats, a distance of some two hundred miles. At its widest, near the mouth of the Potomac River, it is some 30 miles wide, but for most of its length, it is generally less than 10 miles wide. The distance from Annapolis, in the middle of the bay on the western shore, to Kent Island, on the Eastern Shore, is approximately five miles. The bay's deepest point, east of Annapolis, measures 174 feet, and though its average depth is about 21 feet, in most places along its extensive shoreline, a person standing 6 feet tall can comfortably wade 100 feet or more offshore before the water level covers their head.[7] When strong winds blow across shallow water, the only place the water can go is up. Therefore, the bay's waters are quite choppy compared to similarly sized but deeper bodies of water.

The area of the bay has been increasing for over a century. While sea-level rise is occurring nearly worldwide, the Chesapeake's waters have also been rising as a result of subsidence of the Eastern Shore. The slowly sinking land allows the bay to swallow tidal flats and marshes. Some islands

A map of Chesapeake Bay place names. *Author's collection.*

at mid-bay—Sharps Island, for instance—that were once inhabited are now almost entirely submerged.

Water circulation throughout the Chesapeake Bay is rather complex. In general, it is primarily driven by the movement of fresh water from the north and salt water from the south via tides. The ebb and flow of tides, as well as the flow of currents from all the river water entering the bay, creates an extensive mixing zone, circulating the nutrients from top to bottom and from north to south. Currents from rivers flowing into the bay, as well as from tidal influences, affect the formation and movement of the ice and can also accelerate the breakup. However, tidal currents in the bay are relatively weak (generally less than two knots or about one meter per second).

Since the bay's water is brackish (a mixture of seawater and fresh water), its average salinity is approximately fifteen parts per thousand, but it varies considerably from south to north. Salinity is a measure of the amount of dissolved salts in the water, usually expressed in parts per thousand (ppt). Pure seawater has a salinity of 30.0 to 35.0 ppt. At the top of the bay, the salinity is near 0.0—0.5 ppt where the Susquehanna River enters the bay. At mid-bay, the salinity varies between 0.5 ppt and about 20.0 ppt. During times of drought, the brackish bay water may exceed 20.0 ppt at the mouth of the Patuxent River (near mid-bay), for instance, but when rainfall is ample, the average salinity of the entire bay is rarely as high as 12.0 ppt. At the bottom of the bay, where the bay's waters enter the Atlantic Ocean, salinity is typically between 25.0 and 30.0 ppt.[8]

Since fresh water is less dense than salt water, the bay's salinity increases with its depth. Denser seawater moves up the bay, along its bottom on tidal currents, and less dense fresh water that enters the bay from its rivers and streams flows southward toward the sea along layers of water close to the surface. These two layers are separated by an energetic mixing zone known as the pycnocline. The stratification between the salty and freshwater layers is highest during spring due to heavy rainstorms and melting snowpacks. As the summer weather heats up, so does the bay's surface water. Therefore, the stratification is maintained, but in autumn, as the surface water cools much faster than the deeper water and begins to sink, mixing readily occurs. If a strong cold front barrels through the bay area on a fall day, the mixing may be appreciable from one day to the next. By mid- to late winter, however, the gradation between the surface and deeper waters is only marginally different.[9]

The salinity at any given location will also vary from season to season and year to year. It is most affected by the amount of fresh water flowing through the bay as a result of rainfall and melting snow. Thus, the bay is least salty in spring and saltiest in late summer and early autumn. Because over 85 percent of the fresh water enters the bay from its northern and western tributaries, the eastern portion of the bay is saltier than the western bay.

Over two hundred species of finned fish are found in the Chesapeake Bay, but only about twenty-five of these species are year-round residents. Most of the bay is used as a juvenile nursery and/or a migratory feeding ground. Extremes in water temperature, ice cover and salinity take a toll on fish and other wildlife that thrive in the estuary. However, the permanent residents can tolerate a wide range of conditions, and while their numbers may fluctuate, they are able to adapt to most natural changes. Nonetheless, during abnormally cold winters, the bay's celebrated blue crabs may suffer mortality rates of 30 to 35 percent. Oysters can also be hit hard by winter's cold. But pollution, disease, sediment and overfishing have hit harder and are seriously affecting the health of the Chesapeake Bay. In the early 1600s, the bay's multitude of oysters could filter its waters in a little over three days. By the early 1800s, oysters, clams and other shellfish could filter all the bay's water in perhaps two weeks' time. Today, the job takes two years. Oysters are, by far, the best filterers, but today, perhaps only 1 percent of the oysters from two hundred years ago remain.[10]

Nearly 18 million people live within the confines of the bay's drainage area—conceivably 17 million more than in 1820. It is estimated that 10 million people live on or near (within a short drive of) the bay's shores. Runoff from rainfall carries thousands of tons of pollutants into the Chesapeake Bay with each storm. The bay is no longer capable of naturally filtering all this pollution. Regardless, it is still one of the nation's most productive bodies of water and a national treasure in terms of its commercial value, recreational activities and rich history.[11]

In the bay region, snowfall and the freezing of ponds and streams are a feature of the winter season—but not every winter season. The Chesapeake Bay happens to straddle a climate zone where, to its north, snow and ice are always expected, and to its south, it is a novelty. Because a large blizzard or prolonged period of bitter cold weather is not an every-year event, when such a storm occurs or if the bay freezes over, it garners considerable attention.

Average minimum temperatures throughout the bay region average below freezing during the coldest weeks of winter. Since most winters experience periods of a few days or longer when even the maximum temperature fails to exceed the freezing point, ice is not an uncommon feature on the waters of the Chesapeake, especially its northern reaches and shallower inlets and harbors.

The coldest winters on the Chesapeake Bay—its iciest winters—are the emphasis of this book. Ice first forms in the northern extremities of the upper bay—in the Elk and Northeast Rivers. This is where the ice remains during most winters. During some years, however, ice clogs the upper bay and becomes remarkable in the mid-bay. During severe winters, ice is prominent throughout the mid-bay for a minimum of two weeks. In exceptionally cold winters, ice covers the bay all the way to the mouth of the Potomac River and in the tributaries of the lower bay. But during the rare and, indeed, epic cold winters, ice is observed well into the lower Chesapeake Bay as well as its tributaries—at least 75 percent of the bay's waters are covered in ice during these winters for a period of two weeks or more.

2
FREEZING OF THE BAY'S WATERS

How many lessons of faith and beauty we should lose
if there were no winter in our year!
—Thomas Wentworth Higginson

B efore exploring the years when ice was noteworthy in the bay and an everyday conversation for folks living on its shores or off its fertile waters, some words about how ice forms might be useful. Because oxygen and hydrogen molecules bond in a certain way, water has several seemingly unusual properties. One such property is the rather mysterious way in which it freezes. In the book of Job, Elihu states, "Out of the south comes the storm, and out of the north the cold. From the breath of God, ice is made, and the expanse of the waters is frozen."[12]

For fresh water (salt water will be mentioned later) to change to ice, it must be cooled to 32° Fahrenheit (0° Celsius), which means it must lose heat. Heat is lost when the temperature of the air is lower than the temperature of the water. Once a layer of ice forms, its thickness increases when the water that meets the newly formed ice also reaches the freezing point.[13]

Nearly all substances we are familiar with become denser when they are in a frozen state, as their molecules are packed closer together. However, when the temperature of fresh water falls below 39° Fahrenheit, the molecules actually begin to expand. At this temperature, water reaches its maximum density; it can continue to cool, but when it does, it will become less dense.

In essence, the bonding force that initiates the formation of an ice crystal lattice acts to move liquid molecules outward. So, ice is less dense than liquid water and, thus, floats on top of it. This is the reason ice does not form on river bottoms. Because denser water, having a higher freezing point, lies at the bottom of water bodies, ice rarely forms there unless the pond or stream is quite shallow. Fish and other aquatic life can survive the winter without having to thaw out as the weather warms because of this. In fact, if water behaved like other substances, once frozen, it would remain at the bottom of lakes and rivers well into spring.[14]

Seawater is denser than fresh water since the dissolved salts add to its mass. Ocean water, having a salinity of 34 ppt, typically will not freeze until the water temperature drops to 28.5° Fahrenheit.[15] Once the ocean water mixes with the Chesapeake Bay's brackish water (in the lower bay, the salinity is approximately 25 ppt), the freezing point approaches 30° Fahrenheit. In the mid-bay, where the water is not as salty, the freezing point may be closer to 31° Fahrenheit.

The brackish water in the southern portion of the lower bay behaves quite differently than the fresh water of the northern portion of the upper bay. Its maximum density is not reached until the water temperature falls several degrees below the freezing point. As a result, in the lower bay, the entire column of brackish water, from top to bottom, must be sufficiently cooled before ice can form.

Prolonged cold is necessary for ice to form over wide areas of the open Chesapeake Bay. In winters when ice cover is a persistent feature, the air temperature's departure from normal in the vicinity of the bay is often -4° Fahrenheit or more (based on the most recent thirty-year period). In the winter of 1976–77, the difference in temperature between December and February was approximately -5° Fahrenheit.[16] However, icing is enhanced when air temperatures during the autumn months are also colder than normal. Chilly Octobers and Novembers precool the water, enabling the bay's surface to more readily freeze when polar air arrives. See chapter 15 for more about the winter of 1976–77.

Though the long, cold winters were particularly hard for early settlers, even in mild winters, ice will form on the bay—especially the upper bay—if a bitter bout of short-lived polar air, sometimes termed the Siberian Express, plows into the Mid-Atlantic region. The jet stream configuration that permits the Siberian Express pattern to take hold is, of course, a more common feature during the coldest winters, but a pronounced equatorward dip in the jet stream can also occur in a relatively mild winter. When such a dip occurs, if the bay's waters were precooled during autumn or an early winter cold snap, ice can quickly form and may draw considerable attention.

As we will see in the chapters that follow, ice not only impacts navigation and fishing—on occasion, bringing commerce to a near halt—but ships and lighthouses may also capsize from the tremendous pressure exerted by ice floes, and the weight of ice on structures like buoys can submerge them. Moreover, ice on a rising tide can lift a well-anchored pier off its mooring.

3
EARLY EUROPEANS IN THE BAY

And tells the World there is a Land now found
That all Earth's Globe can't parallel its Ground.[17]

Before the first European explorer landed in the Chesapeake Bay region—likely Captain Giovanni da Verrazzano in 1524—a number of different Native tribes lived in the bay environs. The dominant group were Algonquian speakers known collectively as the Powhatan tribes.[18] It is thought that *Chesapeake* is derived from *chesepiooc* or *kchesepiock*, an Algonquian word referring to a piece of land or perhaps a village along a large river. Another interpretation mentions that the bay's current name is from *tschischiwapeki*, meaning "salted bay" or "standing water."[19] Although spellings and pronunciations vary, even four hundred years ago, the Chesapeake Bay was known to be a great and, indeed, special body of water by Natives and Europeans alike. Verrazzano entered what is now Chincoteague Bay on the Atlantic side of the Eastern Shore, where he and his crew of fifty penetrated the forests and marshland for eight miles or so before turning back.

It is claimed by some that the Spaniard Pedro Menéndez de Avilés, founder of St. Augustine, was the first European to actually sail into the bay itself sometime in 1566.[20] Ostensibly dissatisfied with the meager fare the Chesapeake offered that could in no way compete with the delicacies he encountered in his native Spain or on voyages to Peru and terrified by the behavior of the area's aboriginal inhabitants, the Spaniard gave up on the bay and its shallow waters and unfriendly natives, and he departed for lands more welcoming. However, the Spanish likely maintained a presence in the Chesapeake until perhaps 1588 before giving it up completely.[21]

Captain Bartholomew Gilbert of England ventured into the Chesapeake Bay in 1603.[22] The captain and his little party aboard a relatively small fifty-ton vessel were looking for Sir Walter Raleigh's colony when they were driven into the mouth of a great bay by a fierce summer storm. Sailing along the Eastern Shore, they dropped anchor in the vicinity of present-day Crisfield, Maryland. A horrifying encounter with Natives took Bartholomew's life, ending this brief excursion into the bay's waters and leaving the remainder of his crew with little doubt about the fate of Sir Walter Raleigh's incipient colony.

Captain John Smith, credited with founding the settlement of Jamestown in 1607, explored the Chesapeake Bay for two years. After returning to England in 1609, when he was badly burned, Smith never again returned to North America. Instead, he penned papers describing the "wealths" he discovered in and around the great Chesapeake—a "goodly bay."[23]

> There is but one entrance by sea into this country, and that is at the mouth of a very goodly bay, 18 or 20 miles broad.... Within is a country that may have the prerogative over the most pleasant places known, for large and pleasant navigable rivers, heaven and earth never agreed better to frame a place for man's habitation.[24]

With such an endorsement, it is not surprising that Englishmen and other Europeans who wished to settle in America looked to the Chesapeake Bay, the land of pleasant living.

Some twenty-five years later, the following passage was written to acknowledge that the baron of Baltimore and his heirs "were constituted the true and absolute lords and proprietaries" of the colony of Maryland.[25] It initially appeared in a pamphlet (1635) for English citizens who were contemplating moving to the new continent. The Chesapeake Bay and its environs were described as follows:

> It is seated betweene the degrees of 38 and 40 North-Latitude, Virginia bounds it on the South, New England on the North, and the Ocean to the East, but the westerne parts are not yet discovered....In Summer, it is hot as Spaine, and in Winter, there is frost and snow, but it seldome lasts long....When you come within the capes, you enter into a faire bay that

A map of the Chesapeake Bay, *Carte de la Virginie et du Maryland*, published in approximately 1776. *Courtesy of the Library of Congress Digital Collection. Contributors to the map: Gilles Robert de Vaugondy (1688–1766), Joshua Fry (approximately 1700–1754) and Peter Jefferson (1708–1757).*

is navigable for at least 200 miles and is called Chesopeack Bay, and runneth northerly.…Into this bay fall many goodly navigable rivers, the chiefe whereof is Patomac, where the colony is now seated.[26]

In all likelihood, some of the biggest ice years on the Chesapeake Bay were observed when Maryland and Virginia were still colonies (see chapters 4 and 5), though few records exist detailing icing events in the bay during these years, and instrumentation was often lacking (in many cases, there was no instrumentation available) to document what was observed. Thermometers were not used with regularity until the end of the eighteenth century, and even when they were in use, there were few continuous meteorological observations over substantial periods.

It is worth noting that although colonists lacked instrumentation to accurately record the weather, many, particularly the earliest arrivers, believed that the climate was God's will.[27] If times were bad, it was believed that people were living in sin. In good times, it was argued that providence intervened to make conditions more hospitable.

Once more! Our God, vouchsafe to Shine:
Tame Thou the Rigour of our Clime.
Make haste with thy Impartial Light,
And terminate this long dark Night.[28]

Because winter's cold could not be predicted, heaven above was implored to do so. Some personal diaries were found that shed light on the weather and climate of the times, but frequently, even in outstanding weather years or remarkable weather events, the information provided was interesting but not trustworthy. Before reliable temperature data was available, a letter to a loved one or a newspaper article might mention fast-forming ice. Even if a given winter was generally not severe, if ice briefly disrupted fishing and/or navigation and affected the livelihoods of watermen, for instance, it could get more notice than colder, icier winters when, for whatever reason, correspondence was paltry. In some cases, ice was mentioned in newspapers because it was brought to the attention of a reporter by a ship's passenger or captain. Ice may have been as remarkable in other years, but it was simply not reported.

Moreover, during extreme winters, icy conditions shut down mills, meaning that paper for news could not be produced. During these winters, typically prior to the mid-eighteenth century, weather-related news (how low the mercury dropped, snow depth, snow extent and the thickness of ice) was delayed for weeks or not printed at all. On the other hand, it is possible that in some years, especially during colonial times, an anecdote about an ice-related incident resulted in giving undue credence to a particular year's ice cover.

Thus, it is important to keep in mind that in the 1600s and the 1700s, the supposed severity of ice on the Chesapeake Bay was sometimes more related to the amount of ink the ice generated in a particular year than to actual air and water temperatures.

4

ICE IN THE BAY

1600s

From the perspective of living in a world that is warmer than the one that existed when the colonists first arrived in North America (sixteenth and seventeenth centuries), we can be fooled into believing that nearly every winter back then was bleaker than the ones we experience today. This is not the case. Nevertheless, regarding climate, the 1600s were not an ideal time to colonize eastern North America.

The Little Ice Age conditions that impacted northern Europe were evidently felt in eastern North America as well. Settling new lands at such a time surely tested the colonists, particularly since they were unaccustomed to the growing seasons, which were shorter in America than those they experienced in England and elsewhere in Europe.

Gripping cold tightened its hold on much of Europe and eastern North America alike from around the mid-sixteenth century until the end of the seventeenth century. In England, while the Thames River froze on four occasions in the 1500s, it was observed to freeze over fourteen times between 1600 and 1800.[29] Because the brutal winter of 1607–08 was so cold in England, with the Thames River completely frozen over for the first time in several decades, perhaps journeying to a new land farther south than England made good sense for anyone inclined to leave for religious, social or political reasons.[30] The best time to begin a new life is not when the weather is fair, yields are high and all is well.

In North America, during the first half of the seventeenth century, the winters of 1607–08, 1609–10, 1634–35, 1641–42 and 1645–46 were all believed to be remarkably cold in the new colonies. According to the

A Hendrick Avercamp painting, *A Scene on the Ice* (1625). *Courtesy of the National Gallery of Art (Washington, D.C.), Ailsa Mellon Fund.*

journal entries of John Winthrop, the first governor of the Massachusetts Bay Colony and a chief figure among New England's Puritans, the winter cold in 1642 was unprecedented.[31] He stated that Massachusetts Bay was frozen out "to sea so far as one could well discern," and the ice was so thick that "horses and carts went over in many places where ships have sailed."[32] He noted that the Chesapeake Bay was similarly ice-covered.

Thomas Gorges, the proprietary governor of Maine (1640–43), mentioned in his writings the "intolerable, piercing winter" of 1641–42, exclaiming, "The like was never known by Inglish [*sic*] or Indian. It is incredible to relate the extremity of the weather. Fouls and fish lay frozen flotinge thicke on the waters in the sea."[33]

The winter of 1645–46 was also very hard according to Winthrop, who was likely in correspondence with acquaintances in Virginia. He stated it was "the earliest and sharpest winter we had since our arrival in the country." As in 1642, the cold was felt to the south as well. "At New Haven (now in Connecticut), a ship bound for England was forced to be cut out of the ice three miles. And in Virginia, the ships were frozen up six weeks."[34]

Winters in the 1640s were so cold that Gorges, in writing to his uncle in England, noted the trepidation with which his colonists anticipated each coming winter, "You must looke uppon us as prisoners from the end of 9ber [September] 'till the beginning of Aprille."[35] In a cold winter, colonists realized that unlike cattle in England, cattle in America required winter feeding and sometimes cover. Therefore, their care and upkeep were pricey when compared to raising livestock in England.[36] But there was an abundance of wood in America, in contrast to in England, so colonists could have "Christmasfires all winter."[37]

Based on diary entries from the seventeenth century, the winter of 1656–57 was noteworthy for its cold. It was at least cold enough to freeze solid the rivers between the Delaware and Chesapeake Bays.

It was not until more than thirty years later that winter cold and pervasive ice conditions were mentioned along the Atlantic coast. In the 1680s and 1690s, eastern North America, along with northern Europe, suffered through the harshest decades of the Little Ice Age.[38] On December 19, 1686, the frigate *Kingfisher* reached Boston. Based on a journal kept by future governor of the Massachusetts Bay Colony Francis Nicholson, the weather was reported as serene and moderate when the frigate arrived in Boston Harbor. But not long afterward, the cold increased, and the *Kingfisher* was kept in port by the ice all winter.[39] Freezing cold weather and building ice characterized much of the northeast and mid-Atlantic coasts during this abysmal winter.

John Clayton, the rector of Crofton at Wakefield in Yorkshire, Virginia, gave his account of Virginia's wintertime climate to the Royal Society (London, England).[40] It was written in May 1688.

> *Their frosts are short but sometimes very sharp, that is freeze the rivers over three miles broad, nay, the secretary of state assured me, it had frozen over Potomac River, over against his house, where it is nine miles over: I have observed it freezes the hardest, when from a moist southeast, on a sudden the wind passing by the nore, a nitrous sharp nore-west blows; not with high gusts, but with a cutting brisk air, and those vales then that seem to be sheltered from the wind, and lie warm, where the air is most stagnant and moist, are frozen the hardest and seized the soonest.*[41]

Eleven years later, the Chesapeake Bay was affected by another brutal cold spell. In truth, the winter of 1697–98 was almost assuredly the coldest since 1645–46.[42] There is little disagreement that the extremely sharp winters from 1696 to 1698 were the three coldest consecutive winters of the seventeenth century. It is known that all three winters were challenging in New England and perhaps also in the colonies to the south, especially the winter of 1697–98. Colonists in the bay colony marveled that Massachusetts Bay was frozen from late January to mid-March in 1698 and that the rivers could be easily crossed on foot through the end of February.[43] Over fifty years later, Peter Kalm's writings based on his conversations with people living at the end of the seventeenth century convey that the winter of 1697–98 in America was the severest the colonists endured.[44]

A conundrum that the colonists had a difficult time comprehending was why it was so cold in the colonies when they were closer to the equator than England, France or almost anywhere in Europe. As a matter of fact, the upper reaches of the Chesapeake Bay are about 12.5 degrees farther south in latitude than London. After one hundred years or more of settlement, the expected mild winters in the American colonies never materialized. Both the colonists and the colonizers wondered if America was intrinsically defective.[45]

Of course, we know now that England is relatively warm for its latitude because the warm current of the Gulf Stream (off the Atlantic coast of North America) tempers air mass systems moving toward Europe from the west—the eastward transportation of atmospheric heat that has been released by the ocean. Eastern North American winters are colder than England's because pulses of arctic air are only slightly modified as they push southeastward across the heart of the continent.

5

ICE IN THE BAY

1700s

In the eighteenth century, the Chesapeake Bay endured noteworthy freezes during the winters of 1704–05, 1705–06, 1719–20, 1732–33, 1740–41, 1747–48, 1749–50, 1755–56, 1764–65, 1779–80, 1780–81, 1783–84 and 1798–99. Other winters that were not as bitter as the ones listed above were nonetheless cold enough for ice to build during a portion of the winter.[46] For example, the winter of 1776–77 is noted for George Washington's famous crossing of the partially frozen Delaware River. Also, the winter of 1771–72 was remarkable for the "Washington and Jefferson Snowstorm." The diaries of both presidents comment on snowfall that was three feet deep in late January 1772; it was apparently the greatest depth of snow from a single storm to fall in this area.[47] But during these two winters, ice was likely confined to the upper bay or perhaps the northern reaches of the mid-bay. Keep in mind, in the eighteenth century, towns such as Elkton, Maryland, at the head of the bay, were important trading centers for goods shipped between Philadelphia and settlements all along the Chesapeake Bay. Winters that had significant ice cover brought this shipping to a halt.

During the evidently very bitter winter of 1732–33, the ice cover was so thick and extensive in the Chesapeake Bay that ships loaded at Annapolis in January had to wait until early March to leave port.[48] The weather conditions of this winter were not widely reported. Later this same year, the *Maryland Gazette*, the first newspaper to appear in Maryland, was published in Annapolis. If it had been published in early 1733, the bay's ice would have presumably garnered more attention. Three years later, the *Virginia Gazette* was first published in Williamsburg, Virginia.

THE WINTER OF 1740–41

The winter of 1740–41 was seemingly colder than the winter of 1732–33. It is believed that the bay was frozen down to near the Virginia Capes. On some of the tributaries entering the mid-bay, such as the Severn River (near Annapolis, Maryland), the ice was solid enough in January to support loads pulled by wagons. Farther south, the entire width of the York River (near Williamsburg, Virginia) could be easily crossed where it emptied into the Chesapeake Bay.[49]

THE WINTER OF 1749–50

By early December 1749, the weather had turned noticeably colder. Ice had formed on the Delaware and Susquehanna Rivers and on tributaries entering the upper bay. On some streams that were heretofore passable by horse, the ice, even when not fully solid, was too much of an impediment to cross over, except by ferry. Ships that did not want to be frozen in during the winter left Philadelphia and Baltimore for warmer climes.[50]

Peter Kalm commented that the price of wood in Philadelphia (which he used as a benchmark during his travels) had gone up considerably—a cord of hickory then cost twenty-seven shillings, five shillings more than earlier in the fall.[51] All the wood that could be bought then (early December) was green. It would have to be seasoned, of course, for it to burn best. The wood that had been cut by country folk (farmers) in late spring and properly seasoned had already been purchased by the wealthy and the thoughtful who were able to get what they needed at a better price.[52] Since it was not known in the spring or summer how cold the ensuing autumn and winter months would be, it was a gamble for city dwellers to wait until mid-autumn to bargain for the cut wood they needed to carry them through the coldest months of the year. However, they often didn't have the cash on hand to purchase when the going price was low.

Several harbingers of what the upcoming winter might bring—the bounty of acorns, for example—were used by early colonists. An article in the *Annapolis Gazette* mentioned that residents in the back parts of the Maryland province commented on the increased sightings of bears and other wild beasts that they believed were warning the upcoming winter would be a hard one.[53]

After experiencing moderate temperatures, warm enough for cattle to graze and not be fed in barns, around the time of the solstice, a cold front blasted through on December 28, and the cold returned again in earnest. It was then too late for ships at port to escape the ice. In early January, the cold became so severe that wherever the flow of water was slowed, the ice was fine for skating. However, on the Delaware River, where the flow was more restricted and, thus, faster, the ice was more of a concern. Kalm remarked that near midday on January 9, he observed a horse and sleigh crossing the Delaware River directly in front of Philadelphia. Booths had been hastily erected on the ice to sell brandy and other treats to the skaters and others taking advantage of the unusual thickness of the ice. Unexpectedly, a huge slab of ice broke off and began to flow with the current. Everyone aboard the ice skedaddled, and fortunately, there were no casualties.[54]

According to Kalm, skating seemed to be the primary pastime, particularly of the youth, although even men thirty years of age and older were frequently seen on the ice whenever conditions permitted.[55] As we will see in the following pages, not all such excursions on the ice ended well. See chapter 13 for more about ice skating.

By mid-January, a thaw had quickly eroded the ice, allowing ships to leave harbor. Because nothing further is mentioned about ice this winter by Kalm, it is likely that in 1749–50, winter, while arriving early in the Chesapeake and Delaware Bays, also departed early.[56]

Other icy winters were occasionally mentioned in death notices. For example, during the second week of January 1761, the *Maryland Gazette* reported that "a young man whose name was John Sanders, in attempting to cross West River on the ice, fell in and was drowned."[57]

Iciness was also remarked on when property was surveyed. The following, for instance, came from Baltimore, Maryland, during the winter of 1772:

> *A deposition made by Egbert Henderson of Fells point Baltimore Town who being duly sworn on the Holy Evangelists May 16, 1785 deposeth, that some time in the month of January or February 1772, according to the best of his recollection, he did, at the desire of Mr. Nathaniel Smith of Baltimore Town, attend him in making a survey of a lot or tract of sunken land adjoining to Bonds marsh or Island at the Mouth of Jones's falls in the Bason of Baltimore.*
>
> *Surveyor to J. Nathaniel Smith, this deponent further sayeth that he is certain the whole of the survey then made was run round with the chain and compass and that the whole space of the resurvey was at that time covered over with ice, the island called Bonds Marsh excepted, this deponent further sayeth that he does not believe the survey then made could have been executed save on the ice without either wading or having the assistance of boats.*[58]

THE WINTER OF 1779–80

During the winter of 1779–80, as General George Washington, in command of the Continental army, was encamped at Morristown, New Jersey, persistently cold weather shut down the war effort and seriously threatened Washington's malnourished troops. The Mid-Atlantic region faced some of the coldest air felt by its inhabitants in forty years. For the only time in recorded history, all of New York Harbor was frozen over for several consecutive weeks. New Yorkers were able to safely walk the five miles from Manhattan Island to Staten Island. Farther south, Baltimore Harbor was covered with ice for much of January and February. It was not until March 9 that the harbor reopened. Ostensibly, some residents of Annapolis ventured out on the ice of the bay to walk all the way to the western shore at Kent Island, approximately five miles. Several sleighs traversed the ice (reported to be six inches thick) from Baltimore to Annapolis, and carts and carriages crossed the bay from Annapolis to Poplar Island. Solid ice was observed at the mouth of the Potomac River and even in the southern arms of the bay. For the first time in memory—as well as in written records—rivers in southern Virginia froze over. Thus, loaded wagons were able to move goods over the frozen James River, just below Williamsburg. Waterways leading to the Port of Norfolk were crossed on foot by soldiers (colonists). Just to the east, Delaware Bay was also frozen; ports in the state of Delaware were icebound until early March.[59]

THE WINTER OF 1783–84

This winter in the Mid-Atlantic region was thought to have been even more debilitating than the winter of 1779–80 and possibly the cruelest of the eighteenth century. The ice and cold had an impact on the inhabitants' well-being and food supply and even played a role in the price of crops that had already been harvested and stored but not yet sold. In a letter from Alexander Hamilton to James Brown (and company), dated March 10, 1784, Hamilton made the following remarks.[60]

> *This has been the most severe winter known since the year 1740. The rivers have been all froze up since 1ˢᵗ January and it continued snow on the ground. Tobacco has rose in price, it's now at 35 and 40, all cash, and the planters refuse to take these prices. They expect 50 and some 60 pCt.*

If these prices, now giving, continue, the people who are willing may pay part of their debts, but I am affraid nothing but law will make them do it. When the weather permitts the getting tobacco layd [in] warehouses, I shall be better able to judge of the inclinations of the debtors to pay. Collecting debts in this world was, att all times, a very fatiguing as well as a dissagreeable business, it is now greatly more so.[61]

The bay and nearly all the rivers that feed it were choked with ice. Baltimore Harbor was locked up by January 24, and ships could not enter or leave the harbor for nearly two months, until March 19—and then only with the aid of workers cutting ice. Several adventurous men, including Joseph Clark, the architect who designed the Maryland State House's dome in Annapolis, skated on the ice from their homes in Baltimore all the way to Annapolis (some thirty miles).[62]

A number of vessels were lost while they attempted to reach ports in Norfolk, Annapolis and Baltimore. In fact, one way to assess the severity of a season's ice is to determine the number of large ships lost during the winter. During the hard winter of 1783–84, at least five vessels, three of which were schooners, sank in the icy waters of the lower Chesapeake Bay area. Several others were "hulled" by the ice at their anchorage.[63]

Annapolis Harbor finally opened on March 5.[64] Since harbors farther north, such as Baltimore and Havre de Grace, were still iced in at this time, Annapolis served as the port of entry for goods and supplies intended for these cities and even for ports on major tributaries, such as Alexandria, Virginia.[65] Baltimore's harbor remained closed until about March 20.

Correspondence indicates that the entire Chesapeake Bay was frozen to where it entered the Atlantic Ocean. Both Thomas Jefferson and James Madison, in letters to each other, commented on the difficulty of the winter's snow and bitter cold. When the ice thawed, it did so violently. During a breakup in late January, widespread damage was caused (at least three of the shipwrecks mentioned above occurred during this thaw) along the James River, near Richmond.

Along the Potomac River during the winter's final thaw in mid-March, damage was reported to be severe, particularly upriver.[66] A correspondent from Alexandria, Virginia, wrote on March 18:

Sunday last, the ice on the river Potowmack [sic] began to break up, and, on Monday, ran very rapid, exhibiting an appearance of such vast bodies of ice and timber as was never known by the oldest inhabitants here. Our apprehensions for the shipping, wharves and stores were great; but luckily, neither have received much damage, and we are in hopes the river will soon be clear. We hear that much damage has been done at Georgetown by the breaking up of ice in this river.[67]

Most business came to a halt during this time. A new storeowner, Henry Johnson, explained to his correspondents what the freezing of Baltimore Harbor meant to the city:

Our trade at present being chiefly with the country round us here consequently the demand for goods is not so great, as our dependence is on our Eastern and Western Shore trade by water that being finished on accot of the ice, making business dull at present. Trade is at present dull owing to our trade by water being stopt in consequence of the rivers being froze up, which is our greatest support, our trade by land being trifling to the other.[68]

Later during the winter, Johnson was more circumspect about the financial aspects of the big freeze up: "I have no news to communicate to you, except the scarcity of cash which is horrible—a bank is on foot to be established here by May next—if that should take place, I am in hopes we shall do better. It will give us nearly all the bay trade."[69]

When March arrived, boats were still stuck in the thick ice, and Johnson's business tanked; he was running out of patience. On March 8, he commented to a business associate:

I have to say you are a hell of a fellow for swearing. Have not I wrote you every post that we are froze up, and no business is doing here, in that case how the devil can I give you a price current. I wish to God the ice would go that we might have somebody to purchase then we should know what goods are worth. Tell your correspondents that all the business is done by water at Balto. The instant the harbour is froze up and trade is totally stagnated.

He followed this up by writing: "The West India rum you shipped with us is so weak that one drop more water added to it would make only comfort grog—I expect every morning that I come to the store to see it froze, which makes the people turn up their noses."[70]

BENJAMIN FRANKLIN OFFERS HIS OPINION

The Revolutionary War provisionally ended with the Treaty of Paris in December 1783. However, its ratification by the U.S. Congress, temporarily located in Annapolis, Maryland, had been delayed by a combination of logistics and poor weather in the United States during the winter of 1783–84. Snow and ice delayed the meeting of the assembly of a quorum of delegates, and poor weather in the Atlantic and western Europe slowed communications. It was not until May 1784 that the treaty, signed by King George, was finally sent to Annapolis.[71]

Ben Franklin had been staying in Paris to expedite the treaty process. As climate was just one of his many avocations, he noted with interest how stormy and chilly the weather had been across the entire Atlantic that winter. In his journal, he penned, "There seems to be a region high in the air over all countries where it has been winter." He then went on to postulate that perhaps the universal cold that had blanketed Europe was a result of the Icelandic volcano, Laki.[72]

Franklin arranged his musings and conjectures on the recent unusual weather and Laki's June 1783 eruption into a professional paper of sorts. It was presented at a meeting of the Philosophical Society in Manchester, England, in December 1784. The president of the society, not Franklin, presented the paper, which was evidently poorly received.[73] At that time, there had not been a major volcanic eruption in decades. Therefore, volcanic ash and dust were not considered to play any role in the previous year's terrible weather and crop failures. Despite the skepticism of his audience, Franklin was on to something.

We now know that volcanic eruptions, which are violent enough to spew gas and ash into the stratosphere, can have a terrific effect on global weather and climate; although, it should be mentioned that Laki's eruptive power was not sufficient to deliver its ejecta to the stratosphere. It was a mighty blast, but it was not big enough to alter the weather on a global or even hemispheric scale. However, it surely impacted the climate in Europe and the North Atlantic in 1783 and 1784, and it may have figured into the freezing of the bay in that memorable winter of 1783–84.

But a few decades later, Tambora exploded on the island of Sun. This is believed to be one of the most powerful volcanic eruptions of the last millennium. The ejecta from this colossal 1815 explosion changed the global climate for three consecutive years, from 1815 to 1818. In New England, 1816 was known as the "year without a summer." Amazingly, the average temperature in London for 1816 was 12° Fahrenheit colder than the decade's average.[74] In merry old England and across nearly all western Europe, the weather's disposition was anything but mirthful. The weather was dreadful, and as crops failed, starvation ensued, not only in in parts of Europe but also in numerous areas around the globe. 1816 was called the "year without a sun."[75]

However, even though this phenomenal eruption was the main climate driver in western Europe, as well as in many other regions of the world in both the Northern and Southern Hemispheres, it seemingly played a minor role at best in the Mid-Atlantic region of the United States during the winters of 1815–16, 1816–17 and 1817–18.

THE WINTER OF 1796–97

Before the end of the century, the Chesapeake Bay was frozen again during the winter of 1796–97. In *Travels of an English Immigrant to Maryland*, it was stated that the bay was so frozen "that no packet would presume to attempt a passage to Baltimore, and I was necessarilly detained there about ten days, in which period occur'd the Christmas hollidays."[76] This traveler further commented:

> *After this in the commencement of the New Year 1797, a packet schooner dared to proceed in which I took passage to pay ten dollars to Baltimore. We were several days in working up the bay in a zigzag way wherever we could discover an opening in the ice, suffering much from anxiety and from cold. We had a full view of the rivers of the Potomac and the Patuxent et cetera, and at last, we were put on shore two miles short of Annapolis to find our way onward in the best way we could, for the packet could go no higher up though we paid to Baltimore.*[77]

Around this same time, Baltimore native Joshua Barney, who was given the moniker "prince of privateers and adventurers," was similarly detained due to hard ice in the Chesapeake Bay. Perhaps as colorful a character who ever sailed the bay, Barney fought for his country during both the Revolutionary War and the War of 1812. In between, he actually served with the French navy.[78] Sailing from Rochefort, France, at the beginning of December 1796 with his two barely seaworthy frigates, the *La Harmonie* and the *Medusa*, Barney arrived in Norfolk on December 19, hurrying off to Baltimore almost immediately to see his family for the first time in two years. By early January 1797, the winter had become so cold that all vessels remained in the ice-clogged port. It wasn't until March that the bay was safely navigable, and at that time, Barney sailed for Norfolk to resume command of his frigates.[79]

CHANGING CLIMATE CONDITIONS

It seems that it is a human condition to look for changes in weather and climate (between decades, centuries and millennia) and to attribute a cause. Often, we recall that previous winters were colder or snowier than current ones. Perhaps this has something to do with childhood memories, when many things were magnified. When you are young, you have few years to compare impressionable events to, so perceptions of scale are more easily exaggerated. Knee-deep snow to a five-year-old lad does not hit the midcalf of an adult. Stories beginning with "when I was a young boy" almost always end with the present being a "walk in the park" compared to yesteryear—with the cold being colder, the snow being deeper and skating possible all through the winter.

After the midpoint of the seventeenth century, there was an apparent stoppage of the withering cold that the earlier inhabitants had to contend with. The climate's melioration after the terrific cold of the 1640s seemed to contribute to a sense of sovereignty over the environment, since broad actions like clearing the land must have made a difference.[80] Thus, it is not a stretch to see how colonists believed that husbandry was changing the climate for the better.

In 1771, Dr. Hugh Williamson opined that the winters then were less cold, and the summers were steamier than they had been in an earlier age. He attributed this to the cutting down of forests for fuel and space for crops. The larger swaths of open land somehow moderated the cold northwest winter winds. Thomas Jefferson was an advocate for Williamson's line of reasoning.[81] In 1781, Jefferson wrote in his *Notes on the State of Virginia*, "The elderly inform me that the earth used to be covered with snow about three months every year. The rivers, which then seldom failed to freeze over in the course of a winter, scarcely ever do now."[82] Note that Williamson's and Jefferson's sentiments were expressed before the terribly cold winter of 1783–84. It's possible that Jefferson's comments, following closely after the harsh winter of 1779–80, were a response to the contrast between this winter and the mild winters of the midcentury, when, as Jefferson mentions, "From the year 1741 to 1769, an interval of 28 years, there was no instance of fruit killed by frost in the neighborhood of Monticello."[83]

Even as late as 1806, this theme of winters becoming less severe was prevalent among scholars and statesmen alike when examining weather and climate. Noah Webster, however, believed the greater duration of cold, snow and ice in earlier ages was a result of steady but smaller changes in temperature in the past—greater cold with wilder temperature swings produces less reliable snow cover, for instance.[84] He stated in an address to the Connecticut Academy of Science in 1799:

> *The weather, in modern winters, is more consistent, than when the earth was covered with wood....Snow is less permanent and perhaps the same remark can be applied to the ice on rivers....But we can hardly infer from the facts that have yet been collected that there is, in modern times, an actual diminution in the aggregate amount of cold in winter.*[85]

6

ICE IN THE BAY

Early 1800s

To be sure, not all significant icing events occurred before the days of widespread instrumentation. After polar air plunged into the Chesapeake Bay area in February 1805, *Haddaway's Ferry* became trapped in ice off Poplar Island in the mid-bay. Because the air was so numbingly cold—temperatures in the single digits (Fahrenheit)—the ice was of sufficient thickness to permit passengers to walk safely to shore.[86]

According to journal notes from David Bailie Warden (1774–1845) during the winter of 1811, the waters of the Chesapeake Bay had not been so frozen since the winter of 1779–80, "when the American army crossed over on the ice. Many persons then perished on board of vessels locked up in the ice, which were rubbed and torn to pieces, during the thaw."[87]

A diary containing the notes of Robert Gilmor (1773–1848) of Baltimore, Maryland, mentions the harsh weather of the winter of 1826–27. Gilmor's son Egbert published the diary. It was stated by Gilmor that the severity of the winter, beginning on Christmas Day, had closed the bay to navigation so as to prevent the running of the Norfolk steamboat until early February.[88]

Gilmor wrote:

> *Having made our arrangements and abandoning the idea of a private carriage at such a season and with the roads and swamps we expected to encounter in our course, we embarked at Fell's Point (on February 7) in the steam boat* Virginia, *Capt. Ferguson, and forcing our way through the broken ice between the Point and Fort (McHenry), got into clear water about half past 11 o'clock and proceeded down the bay, stopping a half*

hour at Annapolis to land some passengers, who had business with the legislature, then in session. The weather was fine, though cold, and the moon was near her full. We arrived at Norfolk at about 1 o'clock a.m. on the 8th.[89]

THE CHESAPEAKE AND DELAWARE CANAL

Completed in 1829, the Chesapeake and Delaware Canal instantly shortened the trip from Baltimore to Philadelphia by nearly five hundred miles. Below is an advertisement that appeared in newspapers in Maryland, Delaware, Pennsylvania and perhaps other northern states:

NOTICE IS HEREBY GIVEN, that the canal is open for navigation. The rates of tolls have been fixed so low as to make it the cheapest, as well as most expeditious and safe channel of communication between the waters of the Chesapeake and the Delaware. As an additional service, "horses for towing may also be hired at a low price at either end of the canal."[90]

It was imperative that the canal be kept open during icy winters. So, it was often a destination for tugs, iceboats and cutters when ice threatened to close it. However, as the canal was so shallow, ice could quickly form when temperatures fell below freezing. Keeping the locks free of ice was tricky. One other concern before it became a sea-level canal between Delaware Bay and Chesapeake Bay in 1920 was that a sudden thaw could allow heavy ice to rapidly crumble and sweep down its length, endangering smaller boats during their passage.[91]

Though the canal was only fourteen miles in length (ten feet deep and sixty-six feet wide), it was initially operated as a toll canal, with three locks to change the elevation of the water level. Its peak in terms of tonnage of shipping cargo occurred in 1872, when it carried upward of 1.3 million tons of cargo. By 1938, it was widened and deepened, enabling some oceangoing ships to take advantage of the shorter route.[92]

This canal is likely the only water passage that was originally constructed in the early part of the nineteenth century that, to this day, is a major shipping route.[93] Both George Washington and Ben Franklin were strong advocates for such a canal, but neither Maryland nor Delaware had the money to submit a formal survey. After Washington, D.C., was sacked by the British in the War of 1812, it was realized that a canal was essential to

The Chesapeake and Delaware Canal, image taken in the early 1900s. *Courtesy of the Historical Society of Cecil County.*

more expeditiously move troops and arms to the nation's capital than could be done by sailing from Philadelphia and New York down to Cape Charles and then back up the Chesapeake Bay to Washington, D.C.

Some conclude that the Chesapeake and Delaware Canal played a tantamount role during the early days of the Civil War in protecting Washington, D.C., from Confederate troops. On April 17, 1861, General Lee's Virginians were forcing their way across the Potomac River into Washington just as Union reinforcements arrived from the northeast. President Abraham Lincoln commented that the Chesapeake and Delaware Canal was the Union's salvation.[94]

ICE IN THE BAY IN THE 1830s

By the mid-1830s, while harbors such as Baltimore and Annapolis grew, the presence of ice, even if it was not solid enough to close navigation, delayed the shipment of goods. A new icebreaker, the *Relief*, went into service in Baltimore Harbor during the winter of 1834–35.[95] Icebreakers of this era were ships reinforced around the hull, often with double planking and strengthened cross-members. The ice failed to be remarkable during the winter of 1834–35, but it was significant the following winter.

THE WINTER OF 1835–36

During early January 1836, in Washington, D.C., the thermometer failed to reach the freezing mark for nine consecutive days—from January 3 to January 11. A minimum temperature of -11° Fahrenheit was registered in town, and -15° Fahrenheit was recorded across the Potomac River in Alexandria, Virginia. In Baltimore, a low temperature of -10° Fahrenheit was noted. Ice sealed the Chesapeake all the way to the Virginia Capes and was thick enough to easily support ice skaters and ice fishermen at mid-bay. At least a few adventurous skaters glided along the shoreline from Baltimore to Annapolis.[96]

Although the ice was between seven and twelve inches thick in the Delaware River where it enters Delaware Bay, the *Pennsylvania* succeeded in opening a passage through it.[97]

According to the *Niles Weekly Register*:

> *Business has been very lively in Baltimore during the whole of the present year and notwithstanding the severity of the late winter supplies of foreign goods and groceries were constantly receiving through the noble aid of the iceboat.[98]*

THE WINTER OF 1836–37

In January 1837, it was reported that the pilot boat *Tally Ho* was driven into the open sea off the Virginia Capes. A cold and heavy gale from the northwest forced the vessel out to sea. It was alleged by the pilot that the boat was "so much loaded with ice forward as to bring her down by the head and very much ice on deck, was afraid would have to run into the Gulph stream." Fortunately, the *Tally Ho* arrived safely at Norfolk after being out to sea for eight days.[99]

BAY ICE, POPLAR ISLAND AND BLACK CATS IN 1847

Whenever the lineage of an esteemed family extends back centuries, a black sheep nearly always emerges. The Carroll family of Maryland was no exception. Charles Carroll I (the settler) arrived in the province of Maryland in 1691. One of his two sons, Charles Carroll II (Charles of Annapolis), served as a delegate to the Continental Congress (1776–77) and was a member of the Maryland State Senate (1777–83). His son, Charles III (Charles of Carrollton), was also a delegate to the Continental Congress (1776–81), was the only Marylander who signed the Declaration of Independence (1776), served as a member of the Maryland State Senate (1777–1800) and was one of the first U.S. senators to represent Maryland (1789–92).[100]

Charles of Carrolton's son Charles IV (Charles of Homewood) did not live up to his father's expectations, accomplishing little during his life in Maryland. Considered a desultory student, he was susceptible to a number of vices, including alcohol. He predeceased his father, as he died of liver disease related to his prodigious consumption of liquor.[101]

Charles Carroll V (Charles of Doughoregan or Colonel Carroll), the son of Charles of Homewood and the grandson of the signer of the Declaration of Independence, like his father, was not known for his achievements as a Maryland statesman. Although, his son John Lee Carroll served as the thirty-seventh governor of the "Old Line State." Colonel Carroll attended St. Mary's College in Emmitsburg, Maryland, and St. Stanislaus College in Paris. He was then enrolled at Harvard, but on the eve of his graduation, Charles, along with thirty-six of his classmates, was summarily expelled for mischievous behavior and other misdemeanors. Called the Great Rebellion of the Class of 1823, this was, at the time, the largest scandal in our fledging nation's system of education.[102] Years later, when Carroll was in his fifties, he was finally awarded his degree. This incident set the stage for what would become an unexceptional life, accented by at least one poorly thought-out scheme.

It should be said, though, that Colonel Carroll was gifted with a fair share of social graces.[103] Irish traveler William Howard Russell was hosted by Charles for a brief stay in the 1850s. While visiting Carroll's residence of Doughoregan (in Howard County, Maryland), the not easily impressed Russell commented in his diary that Charles "was a kindly, genial old man."[104] He was a slaveholder but was known for treating enslaved people with dignity.

A portrait of Charles Caroll V (Colonel Carroll), painted by William Edward West in 1840. *Courtesy of the Maryland Historical Society.*

In 1846, Colonel Carroll launched an enterprising business on a small island in the middle of the Chesapeake Bay, Poplar Island, off the shore of Tilghman Island.[105] It is now a mere trace of what it once was, and it actually was never much in terms of its breadth and length. In the mid-1800s, it was unpopulated marshland. Carroll decided that this approximately one-thousand-acre island would be ideal for raising cats. On this unassuming piece of real estate, Colonel Carroll established the Great Poplar Island Black Cat Farm. At the time (late 1840s), the pelts of black cats were in demand by the Chinese. It seems that cat fur was widely traded in much of the world in the nineteenth century. Some traders even skinned the cats alive, somehow believing that the fur taken in this manner would keep its luster longer, thus commanding a better price on the open market.[106]

The colonel offered twenty-five cents for each female black cat that was brought to him, and he then proceeded to take them all to Poplar Island. His agent, R.O. Ridgway, advertised in the *Centreville Times* (Maryland) in late December 1846 that he was looking for one thousand black cats. According to the advertisement, he was willing to pay two cents each for them if they were brought to Poplar Island or to the store of John W. Ridgway in the town of Bayside. It is not known whether Ridgeway actually thought that he could acquire cats for this price or if the advertisement was made in error (the "5" in "25" being omitted). Ridgeway was paying a local waterman to feed them, delivering a meal of fresh fish daily.[107]

This scheme worked quite well, as the cats began to multiply. At first, the winter weather was mild. A comment in the *Baltimore Sun* on January 4, 1847, noted that the bay's water had been undisturbed by the ice that normally formed over the upper regions of the bay.[108] But shortly after this was written, a surge of cold air poured into the Mid-Atlantic region. By January 14, it was reported that the Susquehanna River was so full of ice that the ferry boat for the railroad (near Havre de Grace) could not make it across.[109] Vessels bound for Philadelphia from Baltimore were turned back because of the building ice.[110] Through the end of January, though the ice had softened by then, freights were in high demand, as vessels capable of fighting the ice were relatively scarce.

When the bay iced over, the waterman could no longer get his little skiff to Poplar Island, and the cats had to fend for themselves. Unfortunately for Carroll—but fortunately for the felines—the ice provided an opportunity for the cats to escape to the Eastern Shore, thus ending Carroll's black cat caper.[111] Needless to say, it is not really known exactly when the cats scurried over the ice to freedom; just a thin layer of fresh ice could support their meager weights, and if they had missed many meals, they were even lighter. If the caretaker was paid as "handsomely" as the cat suppliers, he may have abandoned his daily chore well before the ice formed. The kitties may not have been receptive to a daily meal of bony fish and headed to the mainland, which was less than a mile away, at the first opportunity. At low tide, even without ice, some of the cats could have tiptoed their way to Tilghman.

Around 170 years after this unusual episode, cats (of all colors) on one of the bay's islands were in the news again.[112] It should be mentioned that Poplar Island was, at one time, more than just a feline fur factory. For example, in the twentieth century, it was used as a camp (for relaxation, hunting and fishing)

A sketch of black cats on Poplar Island. *Courtesy of Shane Cooley.*

by Presidents Theodore Roosevelt and Harry Truman. During the War of 1812, the British fleet took advantage of the island's strategic location (not far from Annapolis and Baltimore) to set up a base of operations. A horrific tragedy occurred there just a few years after Maryland was first settled. In 1637, Poplar Island was a thriving plantation. At least ten residences were located on the island, and crops had been planted extensively. In late summer, the plantation owner, Richard Thompson, returned from a fur trading expedition—presumably no cats were exchanged—and discovered that his family as well the planation workers had been slaughtered, and every building had been burned to the ground. It was never proven, but suspicions were high that Nanticoke Natives were the perpetrators.[113]

Like many of the smaller islands in the mid-bay and lower bay, Poplar Island has been performing a slow disappearing act. Although the cats and other critters could roam about Poplar Island's modest acreage in the mid-nineteenth century, by the late twentieth century, the island consisted of a few specks of elevated terrain that totaled no more than five acres. Sinking islands in the Chesapeake Bay, as well as other flooded estuaries, are a natural occurrence. Nonetheless, their shrinking has likely been accelerated by rising sea levels associated with climate change.[114]

In recent years, the State of Maryland has been dredging sand and silt onto the remnants of Poplar Island in an effort to bring it back to its approximate original size and shape.[115] So, it is possible that watermen may once again fish off its shores, but hopefully, schemes such as Carroll's will remain a thing of the past.

7

THE GREAT SUSQUEHANNA ICE BRIDGE
OF 1852

The winter of 1851–52 was the coldest in the Chesapeake Bay since 1835–36 and was one of the coldest ever recorded along the East Coast. On January 20, 1852, a temperature of -5° Fahrenheit was reported in Baltimore, and Philadelphia fell to -2° Fahrenheit. Even colder readings were measured at other points around the upper and mid-bays. The first bout of severe cold occurred in mid-December 1851, when temperatures remained below freezing, night and day, for a fortnight. A quick thaw at the end of the month delivered a rush of ice down the lower Susquehanna. Another blast of cold air during the opening days of January formed more ice and again shut down the Susquehanna.[116]

Beginning in early January, a shield of ice covered the upper Chesapeake Bay. Much of the bay remained frozen through mid-February. Once more, the ice was a serious concern to navigation and shipping in the bay, but during this winter, ice affected shipping by rail as well as by sea.

By 1852, railroads had been transporting goods in the Mid-Atlantic region for a quarter of a century. Nonetheless, the rails were not universally trusted to move goods during inclement weather and cold spells when ice and snow were prevalent. Like canal systems in northern climates, many people believed that the railroads would grind to a halt in ice and snow. However, a little ingenuity helped allay the fears of most skeptics. Snowplows fitted onto the locomotives were able to clear snow from the tracks during most big snowstorms. In fact, the Baltimore and Ohio Railroad ran trains every day during the snowy winter of 1830–31, with the exception of the one bitter, snowy day when no passengers showed up at the station.

The Susquehanna River, at nearly one mile across at its mouth, has the largest drainage area of any river east of the Appalachians and is larger than the Hudson and Delaware drainage basins combined. Because the technology to build bridges sturdy enough to support the tonnage of not only the goods being shipped but also the railcars and engines themselves was in its infancy, shippers relied on steamboats or barges to ferry goods and passengers alike across large water courses. The Philadelphia, Wilmington and Baltimore Railroad (PWBRR) employed such a ferry system across the Susquehanna, from Perryville to Havre de Grace. An engine would wait on the other side of the river to convey goods and passengers to their destinations.[117]

The Susquehanna River remained a huge impediment to the timely delivery of materials and mail. When ice prevented ferries from running, everything came to a stop—not only at the Susquehanna River crossing but all along the rail network. Waiting a day or two for passage may have boosted the economies of towns such as Perryville (on the east side of the Susquehanna) and Havre de Grace (on the Susquehanna's western bank), but during severe winters, the delays that occurred became unacceptable. Financially, the railroads couldn't survive such delays, and when the trains were not in motion, the flow of information (via mail and passengers) between Washington and Baltimore and Philadelphia, New York and Boston came to a standstill. The nation's government could not effectively operate in this manner.

In the mid-1800s, the railroad between Philadelphia and Baltimore was certainly one of the most important in the still-fledgling nation, so it was too valuable to be impeded by adverse winter weather. Every disruption was "widely and deeply felt."[118] It was feared that with further wintertime interruptions, commerce and trade would go to cities other than Baltimore and Philadelphia. A railroad bridge across the Susquehanna River was essential. However, a real concern was that the thriving town of Port Deposit, a major depot for lumber that was moved down the Susquehanna River and for local quarry stone, would rapidly decline in prosperity once a bridge was built. At the time, Port Deposit was second only to Baltimore in terms of volume of trade in the state of Maryland.[119]

Though bridge enthusiasts considered the river ice and ice jams an argument for a railroad bridge, there were folks who thought otherwise. They made the claim that ice accumulating against the supports that held the span could make the bridge dangerous and might even hamper the flow of ice being pushed toward the bay during thaws.[120]

Colonel Turnbull of the U.S. Topographical Corps concluded that navigation on the Susquehanna River would not be harmed by the construction of a bridge, nor would it add to the ice accumulation.[121] In the end, Port Deposit's stature did suffer. However, it seems that it was not the railroad bridge itself that strangled the river town's economy; rather, it was the railroad, which transported goods with "speed and certainty" and deprived Port Deposit of its purpose.[122]

A bridge had been talked about for years in both the Maryland legislature and the U.S. Congress, but progress was painfully slow.[123] In the meantime, the PWBRR took matters into its own hands.[124]

To continue uninterrupted railroad service, an enterprising engineer for the railroad laid tracks over the frozen river. This was no easy matter, since along the shoals and riverbanks, ice rafted into plates that were more than ten feet thick in places. In this case, however, the shoals near the mouth of the Susquehanna worked in favor of such construction, as the ice that grounded there in severe winters formed a point of solid support and uncommon strength.

Initially, a boardwalk of sorts was put down over the ice so passengers could walk to their connecting trains on the other side of the river. The mail was hauled across on horse-drawn sleighs. But the railroad's chief engineer, Isaac Trimble, was insistent that iron rails could be laid on the solid ice. A crew of railroad workers succeeded in leveling the ice as much as possible, and then they laid rails down over wooden ties. The surface of the ice railroad was ten to fifteen feet below the permanent rail lines, so temporary inclines or trestles were put in place to raise or lower the train cars accordingly. The work was completed by January 15.

Railcars were pulled by horses with towing lines, one at a time, along the tracks, while passengers were treated to a long, two-horse sleigh ride to the opposite shore, where a waiting locomotive pulled the cars up the trestle.[125] In this way, as many as forty cars per day moved both freight and passengers across the river for forty consecutive days, from January 15 to February 24. The weight of these cars totaled approximately ten thousand tons.[126]

Because the river ice was erratic in its thickness and relief, rail tracks could not simply be laid in a straight line across the river; rather, they had to navigate substantial ridges and ice rafts. So, Trimble decided to gently curve the track in places. Due to its superior engineering and extremely good fortune, the ice railroad was disassembled just before ice breakup.[127] Amazingly, during

A painting of the Great Chesapeake Bay Ice Railroad, 1852. *Courtesy of the Historical Society of Harford County.*

this time, no accidents occurred; all items that were loaded on one side of the river were safely transported to the other site without incident.[128]

The ice only gradually loosened its grip during the winter of 1852, and in early March, steamboats were able to resume ferry service—eight weeks after giving way to the ice rails.

Finally, in 1853, the Maryland senate passed the bridge bill into law. The first piers were erected in late 1854, but it was not until after the Civil War that an adequate structure was finally realized.[129] When heavy ice floes failed to dislodge the piers during the winter of 1865, there was a sigh of relief that the bridge would do the job as promised. Oddly, what the ice could not do a tornado did in July 1866; a twister tore the superstructure off of the almost completed bridge.[130] During the bridge's dedication in late 1866, it was proclaimed that "the bridge had brought the two cities [Baltimore and Philadelphia] closer together than they had ever been before." The first passenger train crossed the bridge on November 26, 1866.[131]

This 1852 ice bridge was an instance in which the strength of the ice, a dose of good fortune and skillful engineering resulted in a wintertime marvel—human intervention prevailed against the forces of nature. In too many cases, however, only sorrow and regret resulted when individuals or groups of people dared to face off against icy waters, utilizing the iced-over waterways as either a means of transportation or a form of recreation.

During the miserably cold winter of 1780, not far from Lancaster, Pennsylvania, a wedding party of forty people set out on sleighs on February 5 to cross the frozen Susquehanna River. Even though the ice near the shore was very hard and thick enough to easily support the weight of the sleighs, in the middle of the river, where the current was strongest, the ice was not nearly as thick. Tragically, the sleighs broke through, and thirty-six of the forty people in the party, including the bride and groom, either drowned or succumbed to hypothermia.[132]

In the eighteenth and nineteenth centuries, crossing an ice-covered river could save hours if a bridge was not close by or if a bridge had been knocked askew by an ice floe. Without question, the consequences could be deadly if the ice was not what it seemed. As we will see in later chapters, even today, people take risks with the ice (for example, watermen tonging through iced-over inlets for oysters).

8

WINTERS FROM 1857 TO 1899

THE WINTER OF 1856–57

While it is not known for any engineering marvels, the winter of 1856–57 was exceptional in its own right. The preceding winter was cold and icy on the bay, but this winter, primarily in January, was unbearably cold. On January 17 and 18, 1857, a blizzard, with drifts reaching the second story of some buildings, coupled with a brutal cold wave, impacted the bay all the way to Norfolk.[133] It is likely that this was one of the greatest snowstorms to ever hit the lower bay, and perhaps no colder air has ever crippled the Hampton Roads.

Temperatures after this storm dropped to below 0° Fahrenheit in Prince George County, Virginia, just east of Petersburg, Virginia. It was reported that the temperature bottomed out at -13° Fahrenheit in Petersburg and -12° Fahrenheit in Richmond.[134] Even at Fortress Monroe, facing the Chesapeake Bay (where the James River enters the bay), the temperature dipped below 0° Fahrenheit (-0.5° Fahrenheit); this is the only time the temperature ever broke the 0° Fahrenheit barrier here.[135]

So, trying to keep warm, even in the lower reaches of the bay, was extremely testing. Edmund Ruffin mentioned this:

> *The thermometer blown down and broken, so cannot know the temperature this morning. I passed a wretched night with cold feet. Yet I went to bed comfortable with a good fire burning, and it burnt out—and as with much*

covering as could do any good—6 blankets and 2 more over my feet, which were pulled up as needed, and also a double cloak over all, on my knees and feet. Woolen night socks and over them a woolen wrapper, both well warmed, covered my feet, and yet before the fire had quite burnt out, I was awakened by cold feet.[136]

Ruffin was a well-to-do farmer. Others, particularly enslaved people, were dreadfully affected by the snow and cold. "We hear that…the entrance of the very fine snow, driven by the wind scattered through crannies, covered all the floors and even the beds. Such a snow storm I have never known before."[137] Later in January, he noted: "The only firm walking is on the frozen river, over which the ice and snow extend everywhere. I walked out more than a quarter mile, and I believe that the ice is strong enough to allow walking across."[138] Two days later, Ruffin walked over the broadest part of the river, over two miles wide, at his farm:

The ice was generally rough, but some spots (newly formed since the cessation of the violent wind in the night of Jan. 18th) being smooth.… The ice had numerous cracks made by the rising and falling of the tide and sound of cracking was heard uninterruptedly.…It was so thick that my weight did not make the least difference to the settling and cracking… But we are unaccustomed here to ice so solid and still more to anyone venturing to cross a wide and deep river that my walking over was a very unusual performance.[139]

Ruffin did not consider himself to be adventurous, but he was obviously at risk while walking across the iced-over river alone. But he knew enough to take some precautions; for example, he made a point to dress in layers and carried a seven-foot-long wooden staff with a headless nail driven partly into the bottom to help keep him steady and prevent slipping.

One or two ferry steamboats that were crossing the James River near Norfolk were able to keep moving because they were heavy enough to break the ice in front of them. But through the end of January, ice encrusted sounds and tributaries made shortcuts for imprudent pedestrians. At some spots, walking over the ice became the preferred mode of transportation. For instance, it seems that most everyone traveling between Norfolk and Portsmouth across the Indian River did so by walking. At mid-bay, it was once again noted that people were walking from Annapolis to the Eastern Shore. Even as far south as Albemarle Sound, nearly fifty miles south of

Norfolk, transit to one's destination was often accomplished by walking over the ice.[140]

An intrepid vendor set up shop (liquor and oysters, of course) on the well-traveled icy boulevard between Norfolk and Portsmouth.[141] It was reported that an especially resourceful gentleman gave a few well-lubricated patrons rides to shore in a donkey cart for a substantial fee; such a fee, once the alcohol wore off, would have been considered "iceway robbery."

Fifty miles to the southwest of Petersburg, in Halifax, Virginia, the temperature was just as cold and the snow just as deep as it was in Petersburg. Both the Danville and Bannister Rivers were frozen solid. A horse and rider were seen crossing the Danville River in late January, and ten inches of ice was measured on the Bannister River, thick enough to support a horse-drawn wagon.[142]

The following passage gives a sense of what it was like living day to day during this blizzard and its ensuing blast of arctic air. By January 29, when survival was assured, because so many were housebound by the cold and snow, subjected to days of boredom, Ruffin mused, "Confined to the house by the cold wind and very tired of the confinement. Nothing heard from the outside of the farm. I have read everything I can find amusing in our late reviews and other periodicals and have been reduced to such poor stuff as the books of *Fanny Fern*."[143] For families living in homes with no books to read, much less a modest library, when they were not thinking about their next meal, the monotony was staggering. In January 1857, spring could not arrive fast enough.

Note: Winters with remarkable ice between 1857 and 1893 are mentioned in chapters 9, 10 and 11.

THE WINTER OF 1892–93

The long cold snap of January 1893 was recognized as likely the bitterest air that had poured into the Chesapeake Bay region since January 1857. It was wondered aloud many times by residents of communities far and wide if such cold had ever been felt in the bay. The Maryland Weather Service reported:

Its accompaniment of extremely cold weather…nearly every section of the country having been invaded by a temperature very low in comparison to previous records.…It is certain that not during the life of the Weather

Bureau, which came into existence in 1870, has anything approaching a parallel been experienced.[144]

While lower daily and even weekly temperatures had previously been observed, the protracted cold of January 1893, which lasted nearly the entire month, made this winter unforgettable. In Baltimore, for nineteen of the month's thirty-one days, the maximum temperature remained below freezing, and for five days, the thermometer was unable to budge past 14° Fahrenheit.[145] On the morning of January 12, the thermometer at St. Mary's Catholic Church in Baltimore bottomed out at -5° Fahrenheit.[146]

Merchants were hit hard by the cold in Baltimore and Annapolis, but the oyster industry was paralyzed by the big freeze. Oystermen suffered from the effects of the deep freeze both physically and financially, since few oysters were being harvested. Oyster shuckers went without work, and the oyster-packing houses were at a standstill. A few hardy tongers busted holes in the ice in order to reach the bivalves, but more often than not, they returned empty-handed. Many watermen had not been able to make any money at all in the new year.[147]

Annapolis Harbor was crowded with vessels that were unable to get out into the bay. Iceboats *Latrobe* and *Annapolis* were required to break a path for tugs with tows. The ice was reported to be nearly solid from Smith Island at the lower end of the mid-bay all the way up the bay.[148] It was heavy enough to require two or three tugs for each tow. A captain who was sailing off the East Coast said that there was more ice there than he had ever seen before; drifting ice extended ten miles out to sea off Cape May, New Jersey. Moreover, at Ocean City, Maryland, the surf was frozen over for a quarter of a mile.[149]

The steamer *Crawford* left Annapolis Harbor on the morning of January 13 for the Hampton Roads, but it only made it as far as the mouth of the Potomac River. Because of the ice and freezing cold, the *Crawford*'s paddles (many steamers of this era were side-wheelers) became clogged with ice, seizing the engine. It was able to restart its engine the next morning but could not return to port until the following day. During these two days, the *Crawford*, fighting heavy ice and northwest gales, burned eleven tons of coal; it started with twelve tons and arrived with only one. The steamer's captain mentioned that his thirty-five years of experience working on the bay, he had never se＿ ＿ much ice off the mouth of the Potomac River.[150]

Conditio＿ ＿ere just as bad in waterways and communities of the Eastern S]＿ In the mouths of the Wicomico and Nanticoke Rivers, ice was seen rafted five feet high.[151] On January 16, Salisbury, the county seat of Wicomico County, was snowbound following a major nor'easter the day before. Winds drifted the snow into huge piles, which made the roads impassable. The mercury fell to -10° Fahrenheit in town. It was even cold enough to freeze wild animals, including rabbits, fowl and songbirds. Because ponds and inlets were mostly frozen solid, game birds were forced to forage near shore and were thus easy pickings. Ducks were selling in town for only forty cents a pair.[152]

Watermen had to flee their boats as the nor'easter intensified. Walking through deep snow and bitter cold took its toll. It is believed that several watermen perished, though a thorough count never occurred. The lucky ones—some dealing with frostbite—found refuge from the tempest in Salisbury and other smaller Eastern Shore towns.

THE WINTER OF 1894–95

During the late winter of 1894–95, according to letters from Henrietta Maria Gourley, the Patuxent River along the banks of Calvert County was frozen over for several weeks. She recalled that she was able to ride on the river in a two-horse sleigh and that oystermen carved holes in the ice to harvest the oysters. The big snow event of the winter was a blizzard on February 7, which snowed everyone in for much of the month.[153] For eleven days in February 1895, the maximum temperature failed to reach freezing, and for five days, the maximum reading was less than 15° Fahrenheit.[154]

THE BRUTAL WINTER OF 1899

Surely, one of the coldest periods in the 1800s occurred during the final winter of the century. February 1899 was renowned for what is considered by many meteorologists to be the strongest blizzard to ever strike the Mid-Atlantic states. The snow depth records stemming from this storm are still in place today for a number of cities and towns close to the bay. Snow depths of thirty inches were not unusual where the snow had not drifted. But some drifts reached the second stories of buildings, and in Frederick County, Maryland, fifty-mile-per-hour winds piled the snow into twenty-foot-tall drifts.[155]

Before the big snow, frigid arctic air poured into the central and eastern United States.[156] Similar to the winter of 1894–95, February was the coldest month in the winter of 1898–99. In the city of Baltimore, the maximum temperature did not reach 32.0° Fahrenheit for eleven days, and for five days, the maximum temperature failed to reach 15° Fahrenheit. The minimum temperature of -10.0° Fahrenheit was recorded on February 10.[157] The average monthly maximum temperature in Baltimore during February 1899 was 34.9° Fahrenheit, while the average minimum temperature was 21.8° Fahrenheit. To the southwest, in Washington, D.C., the minimum temperature fell below 0° Fahrenheit on three mornings; the -15° Fahrenheit temperature recorded on February 11 remains the lowest temperature ever recorded in our nation's capital.[158]

In the colder, rural farmland, the daytime temperature at a handful of locations did not break 0° Fahrenheit on either February 9 or February 10. In Ocean City, Maryland, where the surf was observed to have frozen in place on the beach, the temperature bottomed out at -4° Fahrenheit. Several temperature marks that were set during this bitterly cold month at locales on both the western and Eastern Shore of the bay have still not been challenged.

On the Susquehanna River, near Havre de Grace, the ice was fourteen inches thick in places. Ice in the channel of the upper bay was, on average, about ten inches thick; and in Baltimore Harbor, it was thick enough to close the harbor for several days in succession, adversely affecting navigation and commerce for more than a week. Almost the entire Potomac River was frozen, and even Tangier Sound in the lower Bay was closed for navigation due to dangerous ice conditions.[159]

The ice and cold were particularly debilitating for anyone who made their living working outdoors, which, in the late eighteenth century, included most American workers. Watermen were particularly vulnerable, and February 1899 would test them as few winters previously had. Though these men were prepared for winter cold, it was hard to adequately dress for this powerhouse of a blizzard and the coldest temperatures they would ever endure. When the blizzard hit, oystermen were forced to abandon their skipjacks after they were helplessly locked in the fast-freezing bay waters. Walking across the ice was obviously dangerous, but being exposed to blasts of frigid air for an hour or more was life threatening. More than a dozen watermen were reported missing or drowned in February 1899. For instance, the bodies of five men from the crew of an oyster dredger were found onshore in Calvert County, north of Drum Point; they had succumbed to the elements while attempting to reach shelter.[160]

Because ice cover, even at mid-bay, was not an uncommon occurrence in the late 1800s and early 1900s, the locals became quite adept at preparing for hard winters. For example, at the Solomons Island Harbor on Maryland's western shore, wedge-shaped ploughs were left on the beach during the winter months so that they could be affixed to the bows of tugboats, serving as crude icebreakers.[161]

It is worth considering that after the advent of motorized boats, tugs and specialized hulls for breaking ice, the severity of the ice may not have been commented on in papers and letters as frequently as they had been when boats had not yet been adapted to break ice, since the livelihoods of watermen and bay commerce were not as seriously affected. Oysters could still be harvested if the ice was less than two or three inches thick or if the boats could motor to locations farther south that were not locked up in ice.

Other noteworthy icy winters of the 1800s include the winters of 1830–31, 1846–47, 1855–56, 1874–75, 1875–76, 1880–81, 1885–86, 1888–89 and 1893–94.[162]

9
ICE GORGES

During cold winters, when ice was prevalent on the Susquehanna River in Pennsylvania (and in far northern Maryland), thaws could be troublesome for towns along the lower Susquehanna, such as Port Deposit in Cecil County, Maryland. If the ice melted gradually, then—although the discharge could be quite high—the riverbanks, for the most part, kept the river in check. However, during sudden thaws when the river ice had been thick and extensive, the resulting ice gorges could be devastating. Cakes of thick ice, some carrying boulders, would crash into Port Deposit and Lapidum (on the west bank of the Susquehanna), destroying buildings and clogging streets with massive floes, some reaching second-story windows.

The flush of meltwater would not only push the ice downstream from the Susquehanna River and into the Chesapeake Bay, but it would also push the ice laterally. River ice, which became compressed as it moved through areas where the channel narrowed or where islands restricted the flow, would be forcibly expelled where the river widened again. Additionally, ice that was grounded on the shoals near the mouth of the Susquehanna could back up (upstream) for several miles, eventually spreading out on the lower banks of each side of the river.

Such ice gorges were all too often an unpleasant trademark of the Lower Susquehanna River Valley during late winter and early spring. Other rivers that flowed into the upper bay, while also occasionally jammed with ice, were not long enough or able to generate the discharge volume necessary to allow

Sightseers in Port Deposit, Maryland, in their Sunday best, standing atop the remnants of an ice gorge in the early 1900s. *Courtesy of the Historical Society of Cecil County.*

ice to slam ashore as destructively as it did on the big Susquehanna River. The large rivers that entered the bay farther south, such as the Potomac, Patuxent and Rappahannock Rivers, do not freeze as often because not only are they more brackish, but their water is slightly warmer. Furthermore, when they do freeze over, their wide tidal mouths are free of restrictions and are generally more effective in delivering ice directly into the bay.

People who lived along the lower Susquehanna knew to keep an eye on the river. They knew that during a spate of warm weather, especially if rain fell on thick snow, the resulting snowmelt runoff could unleash the Susquehanna's ice, forcing it downstream at a rapid pace.

In the early spring of 1847, the *Cecil Democrat* (Elkton, Maryland) reported that when the ice broke loose, it trampled Port Deposit:

> *None can realize who have not been present at such a scene. All night, the water rose, driving men, women, and children to the hills for safety. Men in boats went up and down the street rescuing families, many of them being let down from their second story windows and balconies by means of ropes.*[163]

Aftermath of a ruinous ice gorge at Port Deposit, Maryland, early 1900s. *Courtesy of the Historical Society of Cecil County.*

During the late winter of 1872, after a deep freeze and then thawing weather, residents of the town of Lapidum were alerted to trouble by the sound of pistol shots and musketry being fired into the night.[164] These reports meant it was time to flee before ice surged ashore, as it did the following day, busting up homes and businesses.[165]

In mid-February 1893, a Susquehanna River "freshet," as the gorges were sometimes called, was again threatening communities along the Susquehanna's eastern and western banks. The iceboat *Annapolis* was sent to help break up this gorge. While it successfully broke the ice around the abutments of the Philadelphia, Wilmington and Baltimore Railroad Bridge, at the mouth of the Susquehanna River, near Havre de Grace, its movement farther upstream was hindered by ice and by a narrow drawbridge. Because this boat's width was sixty-nine feet and the drawbridge it needed to pass through to reach Port Deposit was only seventy feet wide, the pilot chose not to put the *Annapolis* in peril to attempt to squeeze through the ice-jammed opening.[166]

People in Port Deposit were agitated and anxious. The local telegraph office was besieged all day on February 12, as locals were trying to confirm

An ice gorge at Lapidum, Maryland, early 1900s. *Courtesy of the Historical Society of Harford County.*

rumors that the ice upstream was about to give, sending ice floes cascading downriver and into town.[167] Townsfolk who were living in multistory homes quickly moved their personal property to the upper floors. People who lived on ground floors skedaddled with as much of their personal effects they could carry with them.

At first, word spread that eighteen miles upstream, the ice jam had yielded, and the river was running fast. Then came the notice that the ice had jammed again and was not an immediate threat. But later that evening, ice was rushing downriver, past the community of Conowingo, near Maryland's border with Pennsylvania. By approximately 8:00 p.m., it had reached Port Deposit, overflowing the riverbank and crossing the railroad tracks, which were situated eight feet above the high tide mark.[168] Some of the ice and river water quickly flowed back into the Susquehanna, but huge blocks of ice, some weighing three tons, were strewn about town.[169]

The ice did not always appear when it seemed it would, and gorges were not necessarily limited to but one episode per season. In early 1903, the *New York Times* reported on February 2, 1903, "Masses of ice have been thrown

Another view of the ice gorge at Lapidum, Maryland, early 1900s. *Courtesy of the Historical Society of Harford County.*

on the wharves of Port Deposit, and considerable damage has been done to low-lying property."[170] But two days later, when the largest crush had not yet arrived, some older residents were guessing when it would appear. One said that since nearby Rock Run was running fast with water, if it was almost as warm up in central Pennsylvania as it was in Port Deposit, townsfolk should be prepared to greet the ice in four or five days.[171]

On March 1, it was again noted by the *New York Times:*[172]

> *For the second time this winter, this quaint little town near the mouth of the Susquehanna River is flooded. The great ice gorge above McCall's Ferry, which broke early today, came rushing down the river, crashing against the piers of the Baltimore and Ohio Railroad Bridge and rose in immense hummocks....Employes of the Pennsylvania Railroad Company have abandoned the temporary station and residents are again in a state of panic. All the storekeepers along Main Street have moved their goods to the second floors.*

THE GREAT GORGE OF 1910

It is believed that the most catastrophic ice gorge to hit Port Deposit occurred late in the winter of 1910, when many of Port Deposit's residences and businesses were crushed—even the town's records were lost.[173] Eight days were required by the Pennsylvania Railroad to clear the mass of ice off their tracks. Only the tops of the first trains to pass through the ice gauntlet could be seen from street level after the tracks had been cleared. The gorges were not easily forecast, even though the ice was not far away. Because the thrust of water that moved the ice was coming from upstream, Port Deposit's residents were sometimes surprised by the sudden onslaught of ice.

According to the *Havre de Grace Republican*, steam whistles from Port Deposit's granite quarry wailed, alerting townspeople of the imminent danger.[174] And as the *Cecil Democrat* noted when the ice arrived, it did so sounding like "the ocean when lashed into fury by a storm."[175]

Utility poles of all kinds and sizes were leveled, and a number of structures were ripped from their foundations by the unrelenting floe of ice. Boatmen rescued several families from the second-story windows of their homes. It took hundreds of laborers five days to clear Main Street and to dig a passageway through the twenty and thirty feet of ice that buried the rail tracks.[176]

The following passage from a Port Deposit teacher describes the terror that gripped churchgoers as the great gorge of 1910 seized the town:

> *How well I remember the first one I ever saw. It was a Sunday morning, warm for late winter. I was in the Presbyterian church. During the service, strange sounds came from time to time from the outside—grinding, swishing then a roar and someone shouted. Within the church, no one waited for the benediction, but all made a rush for the doors. As we looked out the front windows, we saw a raging, swirling field of ice, already risen to the level of the churchyard, which was some five to six feet above the sidewalk. We got out the back way, climbed the cliff and so got home. I shall never forget that view of the river from the heights above. Could that raging, devilish monster be the lovely Susquehanna on which I had so many delightful sails. I still have somewhere a picture taken of a group of us in a boat successfully riding the water several feet above the railroad track, while what looked like young icebergs circulated in the offing.[177]*

In the early twentieth century, when word got out that towns were paralyzed by ice jams, photographers were among the first to arrive to

An ice gorge and fish sheds at Havre de Grace, Maryland, early 1900s. *Courtesy of the Historical Society of Harford County.*

capture the damage, particularly when, in the opening decade of the century, postcards were in fashion and disaster scenes were best sellers.[178]

Called the "ice kings" in local papers, reporters, generally from outside of the affected area, on occasion covered the impending surges a bit too enthusiastically. When such a group of correspondents covered the ice jam of 1876 with more vigor than needed, the *Cecil Whig's* editor commented:

> *These Bohemians generally love their todd and are excellent patrons of the drinking salons. Every fresh drink they take they see the ice move and the water commence to rise in the streets and they go forth with flash news to their papers…and about every other morning, the town suffers a submerge and the people, especially the women and children, fly to the hillside and narrowly escape a water grave in the city papers.*[179]

When the ice king returned in 1893, the *Perryville Record* observed that reporters from the *News American* and *Baltimore Sun* had concocted a plan to cross over the ice from Port Deposit to ice-encased Roberts Island in order to interview the island's namesake farmer. They were wise enough to enlist the help of a local resident familiar with the route (Lawrence Paxton). The *Record's* writer stated that these reporters' "faint-hearted and timidly picked

Left: Digging out a railroad from an ice gorge at Port Deposit, Maryland, early 1900s. *Courtesy of the Historical Society of Cecil Harford County.*

Below: The Conowingo Dam on the lower Susquehanna River in Maryland. Image taken during flooding from Tropical Storm Agnes in June 1972. *Courtesy of the Historical Society of Cecil County.*

their way, but anxious to immortalize themselves, gained courage as they followed in the wake of Paxton."[180]

Ice gorges were also newsworthy and sometimes destructive in 1849, 1857, 1872, 1873, 1875, 1886, 1887 and 1904.[181] In the years before 1847, such gorges were certainly an issue, but they were evidently not widely noted in newsprint. These gorges were the scourge of the Lower Susquehanna River Valley until the Conowingo Dam was constructed in 1928, about five miles south of the Maryland–Pennsylvania border, five miles northwest of Port Deposit and nine miles from the Chesapeake Bay.[182] This dam has been effective, for the most part, in preventing ice from building up and moving unconstrained downriver.

POST-CONOWINGO ICE GORGES

Even after the Conowingo Dam was built, ice would continue to threaten Port Deposit. Although the great gorges were mitigated by the dam's construction, snowmelt floods of historic proportions (one-every-two-hundred-years-or-longer events) still cause nightmares for the town's residents. When floodwaters rush into the lower Susquehanna, Port Deposit is sure to be in the crosshairs.

In late January 1996, nearly three weeks after one of the largest snowstorms of the twentieth century in the Mid-Atlantic region, Port Deposit was once more threatened by the raging Susquehanna. By mid-January, almost two feet of snow (a water equivalent of nearly four inches) framed the entire Susquehanna Basin. The snowmelt that followed would strain the dam as it rarely had before. Because the temperatures in December and January were below normal—in fact, they were averaging below freezing in most of the Susquehanna Basin—ice readily formed upstream on the river and in its tributaries.

However, in mid-January, temperatures across the entire basin were above freezing for forty-eight straight hours. In general, snowpacks act as reservoirs, absorbing meltwater and releasing it gradually. But with the rapid warmup, the pack was then ripe—isothermal or the same temperature (32° Fahrenheit) throughout the pack.[183]

Accompanying the January thaw, a storm system dropped two and a half inches of rain (on average) over the basin, most of it falling during a three-hour period. Such a rapid and perhaps unprecedented rise of the lower Susquehanna River caused the Susquehanna near Harrisburg to rise fifteen feet in only fourteen hours.[184]

Ice in the main stem of the river as well as in its tributaries broke apart and jammed at natural constrictions and also at bridge abutments. In many places, these jams temporarily held back the water that gushed downstream, but as more and more water backed up, the ice dams failed, funneling all of this river water toward the mouth of the Susquehanna in a single burst.

The Conowingo Dam measured a flow of 6.8 million gallons per second, the second-fastest flow ever recorded here.[185] When the hydropower company that was operating the Conowingo Dam was forced to release a portion of the massive meltwater or risk losing the dam, Port Deposit was caught off guard. Town authorities knew that some of the dam's floodgates would be opened, but it apparently did not get the message that forty-two of the dam's

An ice gorge on the Susquehanna River. Image taken in January 1996, showing a derailed freight train that was knocked off its tracks by ice and floodwaters along the Susquehanna River in southern Pennsylvania. *Photograph taken on January 21, 1996, by Tim Shaffer, courtesy of Associated Press News.*

fifty-two gates needed to be opened in order to relieve pressure from the grossly distended Susquehanna River.[186]

The spokesman for the company stated that notifications of the release were sent out according to plan.[187] Regardless, on the night of January 20, the ice downstream of the dam, channeled by the huge release through the open gates, found its way to the same places, battered by historical gorges and floods of prior years. Yet again, Port Deposit bore the brunt of the 1996 event.

Firefighters from the Water Witch Volunteer Fire Company, as well as from other nearby fire companies, used every means possible to evacuate the town's approximately seven hundred residents. Through their efforts, no lives were lost, but farther north, along the Susquehanna River in New York and Pennsylvania, floodwaters killed fourteen people. In the aftermath of this tragedy, notifications were changed so that the public could be better warned, protecting their lives and property.[188]

10

BAY ICE AND WARFARE

Because of the Chesapeake Bay's central location along the Atlantic Seaboard, it was an important battleground during the Revolutionary War, the War of 1812 and the Civil War. The citizens of Maryland and Virginia were more vulnerable than those in other states to British naval vessels, due to the prime location of the bay and its wide-mouthed estuaries. In the early years of the Union, since these citizens could not always depend on the support of their home state or the federal government, militia companies were formed to defend their property.

During the Revolutionary War and War of 1812, not only was the bay a point of entry for the British forces into the interior regions of the colonies, but there were also a number of deep-water embayments and inlets large enough to offer shelter for part of the British fleet, the vessels that had shallow drafts. The bay was too big for the relatively small American navy to monitor completely. Although its entrance to the Atlantic Ocean between Cape Henry and Cape Charles is approximately ten miles wide—not the bay's widest point—it was wide enough that, at night, even large vessels could slip into the bay's waters with little notice.

It should be mentioned that the winters during the War of 1812 (1812–13, 1813–14 and 1814–15) and the Civil War (1861–62, 1862–63, 1863–64 and 1864–65) were not memorable for their ice cover. It seems that ice played a small role in both of those conflicts. Of course, most of the major naval battles were fought in the warmer months of the year—and for good reason. During a cold winter, frigates or brigs and other naval ships that were caught in a polar outbreak could be locked in ice for days or weeks—or, at a minimum, have their maneuverability compromised. At the risk of becoming sitting ducks and having a portion of their fleets rendered useless, the combatants realized it was best to avoid such circumstances all together.

The Revolutionary War (1775–83) winters were, in general, dreadfully cold. The winter of 1779–80, surely one of the most difficult in American history, closed channels of trade, especially waterways, and largely suspended military operations. At the time, General George Washington, in command of the Revolutionary Army, was encamped at Morristown, New Jersey. Persistently cold weather in the Mid-Atlantic region shut down the war effort and seriously threatened Washington's malnourished troops. Note that the winter of 1779–80 was considerably bitterer than the winter of 1777–78, which was famous for the hardships endured and courage shown by George Washington and his troops at Valley Forge, Pennsylvania.[189]

The following correspondence came during the arduous days of the winter of 1779–80 and was gleaned from the Acts of Assembly.[190]

> *Whereas it is reported to this General Assembly that the army of the United States is in very great distress for an immediate supply of flour and forage, and it is deemed absolutely necessary to make the most speedy and vigorous exertions to procure those articles for the present relief of the army, and to convey the same by land, the water communication in great measure being unexpectedly interrupted by the ice.[191]*

The severity of the cold and ice was also commented on by the opposition, in this case, Thomas Ridout (1754–1839), the surveyor general of Upper Canada and member of Her Majesty's Legislative Council. He penned in his journal that he arrived on the ship *Buckskin* in Annapolis on Christmas Day 1779.[192]

> *I got on board the next evening but with difficulty, owing to the quantity of ice then floating on the Bay…preparations were made to proceed on our voyage when it come on to freeze so intensely that not only the Patuxcent, which at this place is three miles wide, was frozen, but the Bay of Chesapeake was frozen to the Capes of Virginia, so that many walked over it on the Ice. We remained thus frozen up 'till the last of February. There were twelve sail more lying in this place frozen up with us. We sailed from the Capes the 4th March 1780.[193]*

CHESAPEAKE BAY ICE AND THE WAR OF 1812

During the War of 1812, in late November 1813, the majority of the British fleet sailed from the Chesapeake to winter in Bermuda, leaving only a skeleton force to block the bay's entrance.[194] The Treaty of Ghent supposedly ended this war on December 24, 1814, but because news was slow to reach all of the troops involved on land and at sea, fighting continued on a number of fronts for several months afterward.[195]

For instance, in February 1815, American militia crossed the frozen Chesapeake Bay off the coast of Dorchester County, Maryland (on the western shore of the mid-bay), to attack British boats, a longboat and a jolly to the HMS *Dauntless*, iced in at Taylor's Island. This was the Battle of the Ice Mound, fought on February 7, 1815. [196]

During the first week of February 1815, Joseph Fookes Stewart (1778–1855) was enrolled as a private in Captain Thomas Woolford's detachment of Maryland's Forty-Eighth Regiment of Militia of Dorchester County, Maryland.[197] Much of the information we have about what transpired in the Battle of the Ice Mound between Stewart's militia and that of the HMS *Dauntless* comes from Stewart's account. The *Dauntless* had sailed to the Chesapeake Bay, according to the logbook of its master, James Pearce, to engage in capturing American ships and victualing other British ships in the Chesapeake Bay and nearby waters. Matthew Phibbs came aboard the *Dauntless* in late 1814 with a temporary promotion to lieutenant.[198]

Pearce's log records that Phibbs and his men captured several U.S. merchant vessels in the bay and its environs during January 1815. These vessels included the *Caroline*, with a cargo of stone, bottles and two hundred gallons of beer (a pint of the beer was served to the crew a day); the *Charles*, which was burned; the *Nimrod*, with a cargo of herrings and limestone; two fine schooners; and a sloop with fourteen casks of whiskey.[199] The bay area's farmers, boatsmen and businessmen detested the British because they had been tormented by their plundering throughout the war.

As the *Dauntless* was anchored off James's Island on February 5, 1815, three schooners in the Little Choptank River were observed. A short time later, the ship's tender (the longboat and the jolly) were sent to investigate. The log mentions that at dawn the following day, they found themselves surrounded by ice. The *Dauntless* was not engaged in the battle that followed; however, the ship's tender, locked in ice after returning from a day of pillaging local farms, was attacked by Captain Woolford's militia on

February 7. This was an opportunity to take full advantage of the tender's plight. The following came from notes made by Joseph Stewart.[200]

> *They descried, too, a mound of ice, which had been formed at about one hundred and fifty yards from the tender by means of loose cakes floating into the mouth of the river (Choptank River) and accumulated by the force of the tide in such a manner as to present a good breastwork from whence the tender might be attacked, if the party should be able to make their way to it over the ice. The ice, having been thawed and broken in different places and afterward joined together, to effect a passage to the descried spot, it was necessary to jump from one of the hard cakes to another to avoid the thinner parts, which were unsafe to step upon. Upon the proposal of John Stewart led and led on by him…made their way to the ice mound, and there, commenced a fire upon the tender.[201]*
>
> *After an engagement kept up in this manner for about two hours, suddenly, the whole party of the enemy appeared upon deck and cryed out for quarter, waving their handkerchiefs. Upon this, Joseph Stewart and his party immediatly mounted their breast-work of ice and the said Stewart commanded the*[m] *to come off without their arms, in their barge, which they did through an opening in the ice, and they were received into custody as prisoners upon the ice and were immediatly marched ashore.[202]*

It seems that Joseph Stewart and his companions squandered little time in claiming the prize of the tender, which they were able to do at the war's end. Though the truce (the Treaty of Ghent) had already been ratified, they petitioned both houses of Congress for their due prize. However, the wheels of Congress were slow in turning, even in the early 1800s. It was not until December 1818 that Stewart was awarded his prize money—$42.90 after lawyers' fees were extracted.[203]

CHESAPEAKE BAY ICE AND THE CIVIL WAR

Generally, ice cover in the Chesapeake Bay was of little concern during the Civil War. Nonetheless, whenever ice choked the Potomac River—the watery divide between the Confederacy and the United States—it was imperative that Union iceboats break a channel to keep supplies moving to their intended destinations. Moreover, ice on the Potomac enabled Rebel skirmishers to easily cross over into Maryland, occasionally to raid but also to confer with Southern sympathizers in the "Free State."

In the aftermath of the war, the presence of ice in the bay did play a minor role in bringing one of the coconspirators in the assassination of President Abraham Lincoln to justice. In the spring of 1865, John Surratt, the son of Mary Surratt and a coconspirator in the assassination of President Lincoln, was on the run. Although he was not in Washington, D.C., at the time Lincoln was shot, he was considered a possible coconspirator. He fled first to Canada and then to Europe. It was not until late 1866 that he was finally apprehended. Surrat was arrested in Egypt on November 23, 1866, and by January 8, 1867, he was on board the warship USS *Swatara*, en route to Washington, D.C.[204]

However, in late January 1867 the upper and middle portions of the Chesapeake Bay were clogged with ice. Thus, the ports of Washington, Annapolis and Baltimore were closed to navigation. It was not until mid-February that the *Swatara* finally worked its way up the bay, where it encountered only floating cakes of ice while proceeding up the Potomac River to Washington. Upon docking at the Washington Navy Yard, Surratt was arrested, removed from the ship and taken directly to jail, where he was to await trial for his role in the president's assassination.[205]

After several delays, Surrat's trial ended in a mistrial (the jury was split on his guilt in the assassination plot), and he was released on November 5, 1868.[206] But because the statute of limitations had run out on charges other than murder, Surrat was never tried on lesser charges. In this instance, the icy bay and Potomac River certainly worked to his advantage.

11
PILOTS AND LIGHTHOUSES

T o mariners sailing the bay's waters, ice was more than a menace; it was a serious concern that required constant vigilance. Before lighthouses were put in place to help guide vessels around the bay and its many inlets and capes, pilots and their crews needed to exhibit incredible skill in order to sail their crafts to port. Not a single hydrographic survey or buoy marked the way to any harbor or path into and out of the bay.[207] Additionally, temperamental tides proved to be challenging to the most seasoned pilots. Even today, the most respected members of the maritime community are those who are stationed at the helm, entrusted with keeping their crafts out of harm's way.

According to M.V. Brewington :

> *In the pilot's mind's eye, there must be an accurate, detailed picture of something no one has ever actually seen: the bottom of the waterway. And since the bottom is always in motion and shifting, the picture is continuously changing, something a chart can never be. More, the pilots must be consummate seamen, able to handle any vessel, large or small, quick or clumsy, propelled by sail or power. In colonies like Virginia and Maryland…the men who brought in the vessels had most of the well-being of the colonies in their hands.[208]*

When he first sailed up the Chesapeake Bay, Captain John Smith quickly recognized the bay's potential for having safe harbors and ports of call for

Tonging skiff *Gypsy Girl.* Image taken by Robert de Gast in the winter of 1969 near Knapps Narrows, Maryland. Tilghman Island waterman Ben Gowe follows a path of broken ice made by one of Maryland's icebreakers. *Courtesy of the Chesapeake Bay Maritime Museum.*

vessels both large and small. The Chesapeake is blessed with a number of feeding rivers, many of which are suitable for harboring ships. Nearby Delaware Bay, for instance, lacks large tributaries and therefore has few harbors. However, the bay is not only shallow, but it and its many tributaries offer winding channels, shifting shoals, sand bars and numerous islands for sailors to contend with as well.[209] Navigation was especially tricky for the early seafarers who entered the bay.[210]

The lighthouses that rim the bay have guided vessels for over two hundred years, since 1792, when the Cape Henry (Virginia) lighthouse was built. Currently, twenty-three lighthouses are still in operation in the Chesapeake Bay; seven others are maintained but are not used to aid navigation.

Manning these lighthouses was not for the weak of heart, nor was it for anyone with a gregarious nature. In 1909, a twenty-four-year-old who was stationed in a lighthouse off Cape Charles found his duties to be so dull that he penned the following: "A man had just as well die and be done with the world at once as to spend his days here."[211]

Ice could be ruinous to these lighthouses, especially the so-called screwpile lights.[212] Built with stilt-like legs that were basically bolted to the soft bottom of the bay, during icy winters at least one or two of these structures would be claimed by ice, and more than a dozen could be lost in a severely cold winter, like the winter of 1880–81. In February 1881, the ice extended south, to the mid-bay near Tilghman Island. As temperatures moderated, ice floes began to run with the tides.[213]

Sharps Island Lighthouse (screwpile), which marked the entrance to the Choptank River on the Eastern Shore, was lifted from its mooring as ice piled against its legs, turning it on its side. It drifted down the bay for sixteen and a half hours, nearly five miles, with its two dedicated attendants (Christopher Columbus Butler and Charles L. Tarr) still inside. Fortunately, they, along with the lighthouse's precious lenses, were rescued in the following days.[214]

Their story is quite remarkable. On the night of February 10, 1881, fierce gales raked the bay, funneling cakes of solid ice against the base of the Sharps Island Lighthouse, jeopardizing its foundation and iron pilings. Finally, with little warning, the pilings failed, and the entire structure was plunged into the bay's icy waters. Butler and Tarr were still in what remained of the lighthouse's living quarters, but they were then afloat and being directed away from the shore by an incoming tide and strong southeast winds. Once they regained their senses, they knew their lives were in danger. Even before they were dislodged, they were all alone in the icy domain of the Chesapeake, but then they were alone, afraid and shivering. Hours later, at 1:00 a.m., their frozen cottage finally came to rest in about twelve feet of water on the west side of Tilghman Island.[215]

A dory tied to the side of the lighthouse could have facilitated Butler's and Tarr's getaway, but to their credit, they chose to stay with what remained of the lighthouse in order to protect its precious contents, primarily its state-of-the-art Fresnel lenses.[216] When dawn broke, the men decided to row ashore through a jigsaw pattern of broken ice. Of course, at the time, there was no way for them to contact anyone and alert them to their precarious predicament. Although they were frostbitten, exhausted and did not know their exact location, they were at least on dry land. Amazingly, after enduring such a harrowing experience, once the tide slackened, the men walked back to the then nearly horizontal lighthouse to retrieve the lenses, oil and what books they could save before the Sharps Island Lighthouse collapsed into the depths of the bay.[217]

Butler's and Tarr's captivating story was recounted in numerous newspapers across the United States and eventually received the attention of Congress. For their bravery in not abandoning their post, the men were awarded medals by the secretary of the treasury. The Lighthouse Service praised the men, saying:

While it is not part of a lightkeepers duty to look after wrecks or to succor the distressed, many acts of heroism have been performed by keepers of lighthouses. In those instances, when in doing so, they have endangered their own lives, they have received from the secretary of the treasury gold or silver medals in proportion to the danger incurred, not as compensation but rather as marks of appreciation for their services.[218]

Almost as a demonstration of the importance of lighthouses to the bay's mariners, just two days after the Sharps Island Lighthouse dipped into the Chesapeake, a steamer ran aground on Sharps Island. Thankfully, no lives were lost.[219]

Throughout the nineteenth century, up and down the bay, lighthouses were damaged or felled by moving ice. It was not until the mid-1890s that a concerted effort was made to replace all of the rather spindly screwpile lighthouses with sturdier sparkplug-type lights.[220] It should be stated that the replacement lighthouse at Sharps Island, a sparkplug-type lighthouse that was put in place in 1882, was knocked askew by ice during the brutal winter of 1977.[221] Although it is still in place today and may be regarded as the bay's "Tower of Pisa," Sharps Island itself is long gone, swallowed by the bay's rising waters as the Eastern Shore continues to subside.

As discussed earlier, in the winter of 1892–93, the Chesapeake Bay endured a major freeze up. In January, the shifting ice proved to be too much for the screwpile Smith Point Lighthouse east of the mouth of the Potomac River. Two brothers who were the lighthouse's keepers were forced to abandon their duty station as it swayed to and fro in the wind-driven ice. They escaped in their skiff (secured to the lighthouse), pushing and pulling it for two and a half miles over the ice before reaching safety.[222] As was the case with Butler and Tarr, they lived to tell their story. However, because it seemed that they were solely concerned with their own safety and not the vitals of the lighthouse—and probably because Butler and Tarr were still remembered for their heroics—these hapless lightkeepers were summarily dismissed.[223] The grounds for their dismissal was supposedly that they deserted their post.

The Smith Point Lighthouse, in fact, was sighted that same day drifting on its side down the bay. It lasted two more years before it, too, became a victim of winter, destroyed by an ice floe in February 1895. Just two days after the Smith Point Lighthouse went missing, a lightship (a boat that is no longer seaworthy and on occasion used as a lighthouse) off Bush Bluff, on the Elizabeth River, in the lower bay was carried away by heavy ice.[224] Also,

Sharp Island Light knocked askew by ice in 1977. *Courtesy of the Maryland Department of Natural Resources.*

during the very hard winter of 1892–93, the Wolf Trap Lighthouse, which stood at the mouth of the Rappahannock River, in Virginia, was rudely displaced by ice floes. Its last day of operation was January 22, 1893. The keeper John William Thomas abandoned it shortly before the ice crushed it. This was yet another astonishing story of survival on the ice-covered Chesapeake Bay.[225]

Though, at the time, lighthouses were supposed to be tended by two people, it seems that only Thomas manned the Wolf Trap Light. After weeks of freezing temperatures, the ice had expanded and thickened. The temperature dipped well below 0° Fahrenheit on January 17, the coldest day that winter and surely one of the coldest ever. Readings as low as -17° Fahrenheit were recorded in the bay area.[226]

Like the conditions in 1881—but even colder—a thaw occurred in mid-January that unleashed torrents of ice riding on the tides. Structures like lighthouses were always in the way of these floes, which would raft on one another, sometimes building to astounding heights of thirty feet or more. Lighthouses are not constructed to withstand the pressure created by these masses of ice.

The bay had become so icy that nearly all shipping had halted. If Butler and Tarr were alone and afraid in February 1881, Thomas, being by himself, was lonelier, completely imprisoned by ice and fearful every day that ice floes would smash his lofty home, tossing him into the icy waters or perhaps leaving him clutching onto an ice chunk or a piece of wood from the shattered lighthouse.

With each passing day that January and each time his home on the ice shuttered as the tide or wind shifted, Thomas's anxiety increased.[227] His one salvation was prayer. Finally, after a fierce storm and another dreadful night, he spotted the smoke of a steamer on the horizon as it struggled to make its way up the bay. Fortunately for Thomas, the steamer could go no further as it neared Wolf Trap Lighthouse. Thomas saw this as his opportunity to break free of his dire circumstances. He gathered his nerves and strode out on the untested ice, carefully walking the half mile to the stuck steamer. Though he had to yell and wave before he caught the attention of the crew, he was shortly on board. A few hours later, the steamer was able to continue, and Thomas was let off when it neared a coast. However, his plight was not yet over, as he still had to find his way to the shore over unsure ice. Indeed, he fell through and somehow pulled himself on top of the ice; all but frozen, he crawled the rest of the way to shore.[228]

Meanwhile, Thomas's family was frantic. They, of course, knew he was stranded in Wolf Trap Lighthouse. So, when the fearsome storm passed, his sons climbed a tall tree next to their home, a few miles from the lighthouse, to see if they could detect the light's lantern. Hoping to comfort their mother and other siblings by catching a glimpse of the light, they saw only blackness. They realized then that their father was probably gone. Imagine their overwhelming joy a week later when they found out that their father was alive and on his way home.[229]

A replacement for the Wolf Trap Lighthouse was erected the next year, thus continuing the light's seventy-two years of service after a two-year hiatus. The winter of 1893–94 was the second consecutive year that ice damaged the bay's lighthouses. The Seven Foot Knoll Lighthouse at the entrance of the Patapsco River was battered by ice, as was the Thomas Point Shoal Lighthouse.[230] Both lights, though not dislodged, required significant repairs.

Additionally, ice is known to have caused at least some damage to lighthouses and their moorings, in 1856, 1867, 1872, 1877, 1879, 1882, 1884, 1899, 1904, 1917, 1918, 1935, 1936 and 1977.[231]

12

THE BAY'S WINTERTIME DELICACY

"Austers"

Sometimes called "heaven on the half shell," an oyster can be gobbled up as soon as a shucking knife has pried it open, revealing its firm, plump, succulent meat.[232] Oysters can be cooked, of course—fried, steamed, baked and grilled—but true connoisseurs prefer that they glide down their gullets right after being shucked. It is worth noting that in the early 1600s, the first Europeans apparently considered oysters a hardship food.[233] The Natives were fond of them, but oysters were not routinely consumed by the early settlers unless they were near starvation.

The blue crab takes center stage in the Chesapeake Bay during the summer, but come the fall, it is the oyster (pronounced "auster" by watermen) that puts the king of bays on the front burner.[234] When crop yields were poor, colonists were reliant on the bay's fish and what seemed like its inexhaustible supply of oysters and crabs to sustain them.[235] From the 1600s to the 1800s, fields and gardens sometimes disappointed, but the bay never did.

Gourmands are familiar with oysters for their culinary qualities. However, because these bivalves filter water for their food, they are unmatched in keeping the bay's waters clean. In the early 1600s, there were so many oysters in the bay—an estimated 85 billion—that in just over three days, they could filter all the bay's water.[236] Today, it takes almost two years' time for the approximately 400 million oysters to do the same job.

By the end of the nineteenth century, it was estimated that some two thousand licensed boats plied the bay's waters, fetching oysters. Currently, there are maybe a few dozen watermen who make a living working the water

Oysters on the half shell. *Courtesy of the Chesapeake Bay Maritime Museum.*

with their boats.[237] In the 1880s, in a single season, more than 10 million bushels of these bivalves could be pulled from the depths of Maryland's bay waters—an astounding number. Fifty years later, 2 million bushels was a good catch. The haul in 2017 was less than 500,000 bushels.[238] An old salt expressed it this way: "They killed the bay. Caught the bottom and didn't put it back."[239] Nevertheless, it is still one of the most fecund bays in the world, and no body of water in the United States gives up more oysters.

Settlers learned from the Indians how to rake the oysters from the bay's bottom. Until the early nineteenth century, "tonging" was the way to retrieve this delicacy.[240] But soon, sailboats with nets and metal dredges joined in the fray, and they were better equipped to catch oysters in deeper waters. Powerboats came later, rummaging the shallow waters with long tongs.[241] The Chesapeake Bay was one of the last places in the nation where a fleet of sailing vessels was employed.[242]

In the years following the Civil War, the bay's oysters became one of the more precious commodities on the Atlantic Seaboard.[243] In 1886, it was estimated that 20 percent of everyone employed in America's fisheries worked in the Chesapeake's oyster industry. Two or three railroad cars filled with oysters were leaving St. Michaels, Maryland, every week for western destinations.[244] Oystering was cash on the half shell, so they were sometimes caught by any means possible.

Dredges were first used to bring up oysters in New England's waters in the early 1800s. As a result, oyster stocks there were already nearly depleted when the century came to a close. As the Chesapeake was ripe with shellfish, these dredges soon found their way into the bay's waters. Dredge boats could rapidly clean out the tongers' favorite oyster beds. So, in 1865, Maryland

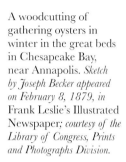

A woodcutting of gathering oysters in winter in the great beds in Chesapeake Bay, near Annapolis. *Sketch by Joseph Becker appeared on February 8, 1879, in* Frank Leslie's Illustrated Newspaper; *courtesy of the Library of Congress, Prints and Photographs Division.*

enacted legislation that permitted dredgers to drop their metal cages in the middle of the bay but not in the fertile inlets' coves and harbors.[245]

Because it was much more challenging to catch the oysters in the deeper, open bay, and because the most productive beds were off limits to the dredge boats, there was bound to be conflict. Initially, in the dark of night, but then in broad daylight, if given the chance, dredge boats (most were skipjacks), would slip in and out of the prized beds with full bellies.[246] Shots were fired from the shore by the tongers. At first, few hit their targets, but their aim improved as the pirating continued. The dredgers retreated but returned with guns of their own.

Catching oysters was a wintertime occupation. If it was too cold and icy for the dredgers to work the waters in New England, conditions were presumed to be more hospitable farther south in the Chesapeake. Even if the bay's waters were iced up, they were passable by dredge boats, so they would drop their cages in restricted areas, knowing that being apprehended was far from a sure thing, as authorities were less likely to engage them. Having a fast, maneuverable boat was a huge asset.

In 1868, the State of Maryland established the Oyster Police in order to help appease all parties.[247] Virginia did the same. Still, confrontations between the tongers and the dredgers continued—some dredge boats were homegrown, others were from New England and elsewhere. In Virginia, the governor William Cameron (1882–1890) actually participated in raids on the dredge boats and took a turn or two firing the guns of his chase ship.[248] For over one hundred years, battles were fought to protect the tongers' surf. The last such publicized battle took place in 1888.[249]

The sharpest encounter this season on the Chesapeake Bay between the Oyster Police navy and the illegal dredging vessels took place Saturday night, in which commonly called "oyster pirates" commander of the schooner Albert Nickel *was killed. The vessel was brought in by the police sloop* Folly, *Captain George W. Clarke, commander. He told the story of the battle. He was cruising about Hackets Point Saturday evening, looking out for the illegal dredgers, for there had been considerable "crooked" dredging going on of late. The* Folly *lay until about 8:00, the captain thinking he heard a familiar sound. He listened, and in the distance came the thumping and the winding of the dredging machines. Although the night was clear, there was but little moonlight. Captain Clarke could not see the dredgers, as they were partly concealed by Sandy Point. He crowded sail, however, and quietly bore down upon them. When he rounded the point, he saw that he was in for a hard fight, as seven schooners and sloops were there on the forbidden grounds. As the* Folly *approached the dredgers, the captain heard a voice, "Boys, here comes Clarke. He's right on us, what should we do?" From the schooner* Nickel *came the answer: "Stand steady, surround him, and don't let him take you."…Captain Clarke called the* Nickel *to "heave to."*[250]

But the crew of the *Nickel* refused, and the battle was on. The other dredge boats tried to surround the *Folly*, but it tacked about, keeping abreast of the *Nickel*. Volley after volley was fired into the *Folly*, and it fired back. One of the schooners that was oystering with the *Nickel* ran up close to the *Folly*, allowing the crew to jump on its deck. Meanwhile, Captain Clarke lashed his boat to the *Nickel*. Clarke knew he was in desperate quarters. But keeping his men close together, he rushed the dredgers. For ten minutes, there was a fierce hand-to-hand fight in which the stocks of rifles were used as clubs. Bullets whistled by the heads of crew members of both vessels. Finally, backed by his men, Clarke, with his revolver in hand, jumped aboard the *Nickel* and forced its crew into the ship's hole. The captain of the *Nickel* lay dead on the deck, a bullet in his temple and a sixteen-shooter by his side. There was no way to tell (at the time) if he was killed by one of his mates in the crossfire or by the police. Several of the police were injured, as were several dredgers.[251]

The *Folly* with the *Nickel* in tow arrived in Annapolis on Sunday morning. The crew of the *Nickel* and presumably a few of the men from other vessels that were on its deck when the battle ended were all placed in jail. But they were released two days later.[252]

Oyster season begins after the summer's spawning months and lasts from November 1 to March 31 in Maryland and November 1 into April in Virginia's waters. However, the catches are largest in the early to middle part of the season—the coldest and darkest months of the year.

The adage about consuming oysters only during the "r" months (September–April) was true for some oysters (English oysters, for example), since their meat could be gritty until the fall season. But because the bay's oysters (*Crassostrea virginica*) discharge their eggs directly into the water, rather than holding them within the mantle cavity of the shell, there is no gritty taste in the summer or winter.[253]

It takes three to four years for oysters to grow large enough for harvesting—at least three inches across.[254] If oystering only occurred every four years, the "austers" would have a fighting chance. But the big hauls of the past have taken their toll on the bay's wintertime prize. Moreover, diseases such as MSX and Dermo have decimated oyster populations, and water pollution and natural silting have not helped their comeback.[255]

Tens if not hundreds of marine animals use oyster beds for shelter, including the bay's summertime delight: the blue crab. In the eighteenth and nineteenth centuries, the oyster reefs or beds (called beds since they are typically flat-topped) were large enough to be considered navigation hazards.[256] Today, few remain, and the ones that do are surely no threat to navigation.

Fortunately, oyster seed beds are showing some improvements, preventing the oysters from disappearing all together. Replenishment is the key.[257] Nearly all the bay's oyster beds are owned by the States of Maryland and Virginia, but they are open to public fishing. The oysters themselves are the state's until they are caught.[258]

Other types of shellfish are also caught by oystermen. Since about the 1960s, because the oysters' decline had been so steady, clams (softshell clams are known as mannoes) have now and then found their way into the oystermen's tongs and cages.[259]

13
ICE IN THE BAY IN THE EARLY 1900s

THE WINTER OF 1903–04

On the heels of the cold winter of 1901–02, one of the most frigid winters in Baltimore's history occurred just two years later. Although some winters were more noteworthy for their blizzards, such as the winter of 1898–99, a number of old-timers considered the winter of 1903–04 the harshest winter in the Mid-Atlantic region in many, many years. The cold was not record-setting in terms of minimum daily or minimum monthly temperatures, but the weather was continuously colder than normal during December, January and February; the average temperature in Baltimore for the three-month period was -6.3° Fahrenheit below normal. Winter precipitation was several inches below average, but snowfall was above average (normal winter snowfall in Baltimore at the turn of the twentieth century was approximately twenty-four inches). Though snowfalls were frequent—in fact, twenty-two separate snowfall events were recorded during the winter of 1903–04—there were no remarkable snowstorms. Because of the constant cold, snowmelt was gradual, and with snow covering the ground for much of the winter season, the cold was enhanced by nocturnal radiational cooling.[260]

Ice was first recorded in the upper bay on November 7, 1903. By December 16, ice in Baltimore's harbor was four to five inches thick and needed to be broken up to allow the safe passage of vessels. By January 4, the ice in Druid Hill Lake (in Baltimore City) was six to seven inches thick.

From about mid-January to mid-February, ice covered much of the bay, from the mouth of the Susquehanna River to the mouth of the Patuxent

River. The ice severely handicapped navigation, even of the large steamer ships, which were advised to remain in port.[261]

At the end of the first week of January, the bay was frozen all the way to Sharp's Island at mid-Bay, where, at a nearby inlet, the ice measured eight inches thick. Just a few days later, with the ice now sufficiently heavy, all sailing vessels and small steamers that were not already in port were locked up in ice. By January 12, rafts of drift ice that were five feet thick were observed, making navigation with even the largest steamers very dangerous. On January 18, the ice cover extended beyond the mouth of the Patuxent River, and only ships fitted with cutters could proceed up the bay, as the ice was, in places, eighteen inches thick. Large and small boats alike were routinely beat up by the ice, and even being towed to port was not without hazard. For instance, the schooner *Henry B. Little* was pinned against the ice off Sandy Point while being towed to Baltimore.

Near the month's end, ice on Druid Hill Lake was a foot thick. By January 29, ice had formed at the mouth of the Potomac, and by February 2, navigation north of the Potomac had all but ceased.[262]

A mindboggling phenomenon occurred on the night of February 7, 1904, during the historic conflagration that consumed much of central Baltimore. People who were viewing this great fire from Solomons in Calvert County, some seventy-five miles away, were purportedly able to see reddened reflections off clouds that then reflected off the ice-covered bay.[263]

By February 10, the bitter conditions had eased, allowing navigation to proceed again. However, another frigid blast in mid-February again locked up the middle and upper bay. Finally, by March 2, the ice was no longer a significant threat to navigation, though ice remained in estuaries and tributaries until late February.[264] For the first time since early January, the Chesapeake and Delaware Canal was reopened. The year 1904 was the coldest in Baltimore's recorded history; annual records go back to 1873.

SIGNIFICANT DEPARTURES DURING THE WINTER OF 1903–04

Number of days with maximum temperature
below 32° Fahrenheit: 21 (14 in a normal winter)

Number of days with minimum temperature
below 32° Fahrenheit: 78 (59 in a normal winter)

Number of days with a minimum temperature
of 20° Fahrenheit or lower: 39 (18 in a normal winter)

Number of days with snow covering the ground: 40 (22 in a normal winter)

Total snowfall:
26 inches
(24 inches in a normal winter)

Total precipitation:
6 inches
(10 inches in a normal winter)

THE WINTER OF 1904–05

The following winter, in 1904–05, was also very cold, especially from January 26 to February 6. In the lower bay, at Hampton Roads, a record low daily high temperature was recorded on January 26, when the thermometer reached only 20° Fahrenheit. Nighttime temperatures were often in the lower teens and single digits during this period, dropping to a record low of 1° Fahrenheit on the morning of January 26. Cold air settled in throughout February and into March. It was so cold that the ice easily supported ice skaters on streams and inlets as far south as the mouth of the York River (on Virginia's western shore), where skating was a commonplace activity throughout the first week of March 1905.[265]

THE WINTER OF 1911–12

Early in the new year (1912), the waters of the bay were icing over. By mid-January, heavy ice was reported by the masters of vessels that churned up the bay to unload or pick up shipments in Baltimore. Ice was obstructing shipping in both the upper bay and mid-bay. Several buoys were knocked out of position by the ice. Some were lying on their sides and virtually useless for navigation. In fact, the Poplar Island buoy was two and a half miles south of where it should have been, and the Sharps Island buoy had moved five miles south of its original position. Two three-mast schooners had run aground on Poplar Island, likely because of the missing buoys.[266]

The cutter *Apache* was kept busy relieving vessels caught in the ice. Several steamers, including the *Pola*, were unable to push up the bay from Norfolk because they were in short supply of the extra fuel (coal) required to fight the ice. They turned back to take on more coal. At least three other steamers that were attempting to exit Baltimore Harbor were secured by thick ice.

Skaters on ice near Hampton, Virginia. This photograph was likely taken in January 1905. *Courtesy of the* Virginia Pilot News.

The ice approaching Annapolis Harbor was too thick to enter, even for big schooners, and no ships could leave the harbor.

Additionally, numerous reports of oyster boats being helplessly stuck in the bay and its tributaries were given attention by tugs and cutters alike. The tug *Britannia* mentioned in its log that ice was prevalent even as far south as Point Lookout at the mouth of the Potomac River. *Britannia*'s captain, Alonso Dunn, said that ice conditions were the worst he had seen during his many years of service towing vessels in the bay.[267]

THE WINTER OF 1916–17

The inhabitants of the bay area had to endure yet another bitter winter in 1916–17. While the cold weather was well appreciated by skiers, skaters and sledders and brought a smile to the face of coal dealers, most folks remained indoors when possible. The coldest day of the season occurred

Piles of ice surrounding a waterman with a log canoe on shore near the Nanticoke River (Eastern Shore of Maryland). This photograph was taken in January 1917. *Courtesy of the Calvert Marine Museum.*

on February 13. The official temperature reading in the city of Baltimore was 3.6° Fahrenheit, but readings in the suburbs and beyond were surely below the 0° Fahrenheit mark. In fact, just to the north of "Charm City," Towson registered -2° Fahrenheit and Whitehall measured -8° Fahrenheit.[268] Temperatures had not been this cold since 1909.

According to the masters of ocean steamers, the bay was solid with ice all the way to Poplar Island. When two cargo ships moving up the bay from Norfolk to Baltimore were delayed overnight because of this most recent hard freeze, it was decided to postpone any further similar attempts. In Baltimore Harbor, the local municipal ferryboat was caught in the ice and needed help freeing itself. To the rescue came the cutter *Latrobe*, but the ice was jammed so hard, even with the *Latrobe*'s help passengers could not be immediately landed.[269] A number of outbound vessels were biding their time in the harbor, waiting for conditions to ease up so that they could make their sojourn southward.

Farther down the bay, at the mouth of the Wicomico River, on Maryland's Eastern Shore, the ice was said to be ten inches thick. Still farther south, on the bay's Virginia tributaries, several schooners were frozen in, and even in the Carolina sounds, ice was a nuisance to shipping—one report made mention of ice that was five inches thick.[270]

THE WINTER OF 1917–18

The winters of 1916–17 and 1917–18 were possibly two of the coldest back-to-back winters ever in the Chesapeake Bay region. The winter of 1917–18 rivals 1976–77 as the iciest winter of the twentieth century.[271] A series of polar outbreaks affected the Mid-Atlantic region from late November 1917 to March 1918. Even in the lower bay, shipping was all but closed for much

A young girl standing on a frozen beach near Solomons (Maryland), with iceboats on the Patuxent River in the background. This photograph was likely taken in January 1917 or 1918. *Courtesy of the Calvert Marine Museum.*

of the winter. Ice choked the James, York and Elizabeth Rivers and formed as far south as the mouth of the Chesapeake.

The cold set in early. By mid-December, nearly the entire bay was involved with ice. The passenger ship *Potomac* was more than six days late arriving in Norfolk from Washington, D.C., because of ice issues. It was basically motionless for two days not far from Old Point Comfort. A young girl who had been aboard the *Potomac* recounted to a relative, years later, that she had seen a duck frozen in the ice.[272]

On New Year's Day, an awful fire in Virginia Beach engulfed the cherished Monticello Hotel and then two city blocks before it could be extinguished. The mind-numbing cold contributed to the seriousness of this fire, as the water supply that was needed to douse it was compromised by the winter freeze.[273]

Ice was mentioned in the bay region's big-city and small-town newspapers almost daily, and on the streets, the ice and cold were always part of the conversation. Through the first ten days of January only the largest ocean freighters were able to break a channel for themselves.[274] All other boats needed assistance by tugs or iceboats to traverse the bay. The icebreaker

Ice coating a building and fire equipment in Virginia Beach, Virginia, following a fire. This photograph was taken on January 1, 1918. *Courtesy of the Virginia Pilot News.*

Latrobe was hard at work again this winter, as was mentioned in a *Baltimore Sun* article on January 3, 1918: "The iceboat *Latrobe* is striving manfully to keep open a channel to all important points." Though the *Latrobe* could handle the ice, a concern for boats following behind was the heavy broken ice left in its wake that only larger vessels could manage. Tugboats, which were normally able to hold their own when the bay iced up for a few days, now needed help from icebreakers to haul their tows.

In mid-January, a deep, unsettling cold set it. At ports in the upper bay, temperatures failed to get out of the single digits (Fahrenheit) for several days. The ice increased in thickness every day, and navigation became untenable. Both the *Northland* and *Southland*, three-hundred-foot-long steel-hulled ships, were hemmed in by thick ice.[275] Other than a few feisty tugs and those hapless boats caught in the ice, all boats in the bay remained in port.

Losing a shipment of cargo could be devastating to a small firm, and many were hesitant to trust the tugs and iceboats to get them safely to clear water. However, confidence built whenever a big warship was seen plowing through the bay's ice.[276] Despite their misgivings, several cargo vessels followed behind a battleship that was leaving Baltimore in mid-January, making open water in just a few hours. After this initial foray proved to be uneventful, a number of steamships then signed on to join convoys. Of course, because the Great War was still going strong in the early days of 1918, there were few warships that could be spared to act as icebreakers.[277]

Controversy erupted a little more than a week after the big fighting ship entered the bay. "Baltimore ship brokers and agents learned that it is unprofitable to raise the ire of the commander of a United States warship, particularly when the warship is doing work not classified as fighting."[278] Apparently, the battleship left in a huff and did not return to Baltimore— nor did its commander notify city officials that it would. This decision was left to the rear admiral of the fleet the ship belonged to, and he refused to allow the big cruiser to return to the bay.[279]

It seems that some vessels refused to obey the commandant's orders to always remain behind him when in convoy. Once in the bay, if there was open water ahead, some of the following boats would circle in front of the warship. Angering the commandant, the offending pilots of these boats did not try to return to the line behind the ship when signaled to do so. In an earlier incident, five vessels went aground when moving past the cruiser. The commandant asked the naval tug that was accompanying his ship to help free them, which delayed the convoy several hours. However, after the third time certain pilots chose not to follow the commandant's orders, he had had enough and simply sailed out of the bay.[280]

Heads had cooled a few days later, though. This was fortunate, as the ice had not departed with the warship—it had only become harder and thicker. The ice ship *Latrobe* was struggling in this heavy ice, as was the *Annapolis*— their machinery considered obsolete. Now, an even bigger battleship was in the bay, and shipping merchants were pleased again.[281] A downside to this immense cruiser was that because it had a larger draft, it could not move as far into Baltimore Harbor as the previous one could.

To give credence to how challenging navigating the ice had become, by the month's end the new battleship was obliged to anchor off Thomas Point with a convoy of six vessels to keep from being swept aground.[282] Presumably, the ice was being pushed by strong tidal currents, forcing the mighty ship out of the channel.

By early February, the cold and ice had an even firmer grip on the bay. As far south as Hampton Roads and Norfolk, the ice was described as very bad. Pilots commented that the conditions were as bad as they had ever encountered. At the mouth of the Patuxent River, the ice was twelve to fifteen inches thick.[283] Fortunately, by then, the icebreaking battleship was back in action, opening channels and escorting vessels.

In mid-February—though the weather was still cold—the bay ice had let up enough for steamship executives to report that oceangoing freighters had been able to reach the port of Baltimore. These executives credited this improvement to the hard work of the municipal icebreakers, the big battleship, the coast guard cutters and the increasing engine power of the ships themselves. Nonetheless, the Chesapeake and Delaware Canal was still iced up, and in the bay, because so many buoys had been knocked askew, shipping was largely confined to the daylight hours.[284]

The icy siege of 1917–18 meant that the watermen were hard-pressed to tong for oysters. Indeed, a woeful harvest ensued. However, there was then a new way to get oysters to restaurants and on the tables of Baltimoreans that had not been available during the icy winters of years past—trucks. With ice thicknesses between six inches and two feet routinely measured in the Chesapeake Bay in late January, sailing vessels, as well as power schooners, remained in port, along with their cargo of oysters. The food themes of the Great War era, such as "meatless Tuesdays and pork-less Saturdays," along with the usual demand for fish or shellfish on Fridays, were being tested, as there was just not a large enough supply of readily available bivalves to satisfy all the bay's customers.[285]

Finally, a merchant who had several vessels full of oysters icebound just offshore came up with the idea to wheel (using wheelbarrows or carts) the oysters in the ships' holds over the ice to shore. Trucks were then dispatched to the nearest accessible point for each vessel, and the oysters were loaded onto the waiting trucks.[286] After loading was completed, the trucks immediately headed off with their fresh-frozen, sweet-tasting cargo to various retailers, businesses and restaurants up and down the bay.

Based on Henrietta Marie Gourley's letters, the Patuxent River in Calvert County at mid-bay was frozen solid for a good portion of January and February 1918. She said that both she and her sister, as well as their old Aunt Lizzie, all slept in the same room in order to stay warm at night. They cooked in a room where the water used for cooking was frozen solid in its container, even though it was only three feet from the stove. When the ice finally disappeared, she mentions that the wharf and two beacons went with it.[287]

THE WINTER OF 1919–20

This winter, the third cruel winter in four years in the Chesapeake Bay region, was described as an old-fashioned winter by the *Baltimore Sun*.[288] Winter arrived early, bringing polar-like cold in mid-December, with a -7° Fahrenheit reading in the city of Baltimore on December 18. The cold remained in place through January.

Ice in Baltimore Harbor and in the upper bay was holding up shipping, as many boats remained tied up at piers. The icebreaker *Latrobe* was busy leading freighters in and out of Baltimore. Outbound ships did not encounter ice-free water until they passed Annapolis. The passenger liners *Chesapeake* and *Old Bay* did not even attempt to leave Baltimore Harbor for Norfolk. Even though this winter was not nearly as frigid as the winter of 1917–18, according to an official from the liner company, he could not recall a time when those boats endured the many delays they experienced that winter.[289]

ICE SKATING

Ice skating was a favorite winter pastime in the eighteenth, nineteenth and early twentieth centuries, when it seemed that winters were always cold enough for skating. Once the ice was solid and a fine spell of cold weather invited people out of their homes, skates were donned by all who had them.

Black ice is the best for ice skating. It is hard and fast, and the skates easily glide over it. If the ice was softer—for example, if snow had fallen just as the water had begun to freeze—the skates would bounce as much as they glided. Nothing could improve such ice except a complete melt and refreeze.[290]

Three skaters near Solomons (Maryland). This photograph was likely taken in January 1917 or 1918. *Courtesy of the Calvert Marine Museum.*

Left: *Ice Skating on the C&O Canal. Courtesy of Guy Steele Fairlamb.*

Right: Skaters on the harbor at St. Michael's (Maryland). This photograph was likely taken in the 1920s or 1930s. *H. Robins Hollyday, photographer; courtesy of the Talbot County Historical Society, Easton, Maryland.*

Folger McKinsey (see chapter 14 for more about the "Bentztown Bard") reminisced about skating in Elkton, Maryland, in the 1880s and 1890s.[291]

Captain Really's oyster boat used to tie up at the town bridge in those days, after making its way up the bay from the oyster grounds, and everybody used it as a starting point for the big skate on Saturdays—twenty miles down the river to Turkey Point Light to see the iceboats breaking up the big fields of ice on the Chesapeake. It was often hard digging to get down the whole length of the river with the wind in your face, but coming back was a cinch because you could hold your coat wide open and practically be blown up the river, back to the old starting place.

14

THE WINTERS BETWEEN 1919 AND 1977

THE WINTER OF 1935–36

In the final days of 1935, as the year ended, the mercury dropped. The new year dawned with freighters frozen in place. In mid-January, when the ice was finally cut through, watermen at Kent Narrows worked for the first time since late December.[292] Iceboats (with cutters), such as the *Annapolis*, were required to open the deeper channels for larger ships. The ice was reported to be nine inches thick in places. All working boats (such as skipjacks) were tied up until the ice abated several weeks later.[293]

During late January 1936, the bay was frozen over all the way down to the mouth of the Patuxent River, with ice being a nuisance as far south as Point Lookout at the mouth of the Potomac River, a distance of about one hundred miles from the top of the bay. Tributaries were frozen solid as far south as the James River, and ice floes were observed in the Virginia Capes, where the Chesapeake enters the Atlantic Ocean.

Temperatures dipped to 0° Fahrenheit in the Baltimore suburbs on the morning of January 28, 1936.[294] All sorts of beacons and buoys were crushed by the ice. Many others were displaced—a few more than a mile down the bay—and rendered useless as channel markers, though a few were still in working condition. The coast guard was also busy freeing boats from thick ice. The cutter *Mohawk* released nine good-sized ships from the grips of the ice off Thomas Point; it also freed a dozen steamers that were stuck in ice at the mouth of the Severn River.[295] As in other big ice years, the foolhardy traipsed over the ice from Kent Island to Annapolis.

People standing on ice off Virginia Beach, Virginia. This photograph was taken in January 1936. *Courtesy of the* Virginia Pilot News.

Baltimore's two icebreakers were working both Baltimore Harbor and the bay. Because these breakers were designed with blunt prows and iron hulls, they could often break through the ice easier than larger, sharp-nosed vessels.[296] However, when persistent winds piled up ice along the Eastern Shore, as they had in mid- and late January 1936, even those breakers had to back off. Plus, in such conditions, as soon as this concentrated ice is broken through, fresh ice immediately drifts in.[297]

The ferry *Pittsburgh*, which sailed out of Baltimore, attempted to reach the Eastern Shore but was turned away by the thick buildup of ice. Since it made little headway when trying to return, the icebreaker *Annapolis* was called to assist it. The return trip took a total of seven and a half hours, five and a half hours longer than usual.[298]

At Breton Bay in St. Mary's County, residents were able to walk over the frozen water to the county seat of Leonardtown, which was more than half a mile away. An unusual sight came when county trucks dumped loads of snow onto the ice of Breton Bay, an embayment off the Potomac River, following a big storm on February 7 that dropped ten inches. Even heavy trucks had no issues crossing Breton Bay.[299] Farther up the Potomac River, the nation's capital had to contend with the crushing force of ice on the move.

Above: The steamboat *District of Columbia* encased in ice in the Potomac River. This photograph was likely taken in January 1936. *Courtesy of the Calvert Marine Museum.*

Right: Damage from ice along the Washington, D.C. (Georgetown) waterfront. This photograph was likely taken in January 1936. *Courtesy of the Calvert Marine Museum.*

Three men working to exchange a damaged buoy with a lighted one. This photograph was taken from the buoy tender *Violet*, likely in January 1936. *Courtesy of the Calvert Marine Museum.*

Cove Point Lighthouse keeper James Somers (*left*) and assistant Charles Sadler (*right*) in front of rafted ice on the shore of the Chesapeake Bay, near Cove Point. This photograph was likely taken in January 1936. *Courtesy of the Calvert Marine Museum.*

Communities on Smith Island and Tangier Island bore the brunt of the effects of the hard ice. Coast guard cutters were unable to get close enough to the shallow island harbors to offer assistance. Of course, these islanders were used to enduring hardships. Nevertheless, it is purported that in late January 1936, a pregnant Smith Island woman desperately tried to reach a hospital in Crisfield on Maryland's Eastern Shore. Friends and family put her aboard the island's mailboat, *The Island Belle*, chopping their way with axes through the four to six inches of ice over the nine and a half miles to Crisfield. They finally made it, but sadly, to no avail, as both mother and child perished en route to the hospital.[300]

Heavy ice cut off Tangier Island, located eleven miles south of Smith Island, from the mainland for almost all of late January and February 1936. At first, a dirigible was employed to bring in food supplies, and then small planes helped.[301] Later, the U.S. Army Air Corps came to the rescue by dropping food staples through the bomb bay doors of army bombers. One Tangier Islander said he never dreamed he would enjoy being bombarded with beans.[302]

Oystermen tonging through ice. This photograph was likely taken in January 1936. *H. Robins Hollyday, photographer; courtesy of the Talbot County Historical Society, Easton, Maryland.*

A driving excursion on the ice of the Chesapeake Bay. This photograph was likely taken in January 1936. *H. Robins Hollyday, photographer; courtesy of the Talbot County Historical Society, Easton, Maryland.*

A car on ice towing a boat packed with Chesapeake oysters. This photograph was likely taken in 1936. *H. Robins Hollyday, photographer; courtesy of the Talbot County Historical Society, Easton, Maryland.*

In addition, in early February 1936, the largest snowstorm to hit the Mid-Atlantic region since 1908 crippled the tidewater area of Virginia. The city of Norfolk was shut down for days by the heavy snowfall. Near Virginia Beach, the Chesapeake Bay, where it enters the Atlantic Ocean, froze for several miles, from the shoreline out to the main channel. Much of this ice had been broken off from an ice pack farther up the bay and had been pushed down to the lower bay, where it fused with fresh ice, newly formed from the most recent incursion of frigid air.[303] According to the memories of old-timers (and newspaper accounts), this was just the third time that the ocean along the beachfront had frozen; the other two instances had occurred during the winters of 1857 and 1918.

By late February 1936, the ice and snow finally began to melt. Still, a three-mile stretch of the Chesapeake and Delaware Canal had ice that was yet unbroken. Once again, the *Pittsburgh* needed help returning to port. The round trip to and from the Eastern Shore, this time, took thirteen hours, nine hours longer than usual. Weakening ice along the Eastern Shore forced oystermen to abandon their tonging holes, which had been drilled and maintained for well over a month. It had been nearly two full months since they had last been able to tong oysters from their boats.[304]

THE WINTER OF 1939–40

This winter was remarkable both for its big snow and for its extremely cold January. One or two questionable readings of subzero temperatures were recorded, but regardless of whether the thermometer dipped below zero, the cold that winter is still etched into the memories of older bay area residents.

Harbors were choked with ice, and a few commercial fishing fleets were locked in, particularly in the upper and mid-bay areas. A tug from Norfolk called the *Naugatuck* was piloted up the bay to keep the Chesapeake and

Mathias Point Lighthouse. This image shows the lighthouse tender being lowered to an awaiting boat, and it was taken in January 1948. *Courtesy of the Calvert Marine Museum.*

Delaware Canal open for traffic and to break a path so that oil barges could deliver fuel oil to the U.S. Naval Academy. The icebreaker *Annapolis* was needed to escort steamers into Baltimore's harbor. Its captain mentioned that the ice was ten inches thick in places near the Eastern Shore and that ice could be seen piled three to four feet thick on the Eastern Shore's beaches.[305]

Near the end of January, a blizzard buried parts of southern Maryland in drifts up to eight feet high, shutting down schools, churches and most business and farm activities for a week or longer. On the bay, this storm forced a 330-ton freighter to run aground on Hooper's Island, across the bay from the mouth of the Patuxent.[306]

THE WINTER OF 1947–48

The winter of 1947–48 was the coldest since 1935–36. A protracted period of cold weather arrived in mid-January and lasted until late February.

Left: An aerial view of the tanker *Ira Bushey* and tugboat *Senator* in ice. This photograph was likely taken in the early 1940s. *H. Robins Hollyday, photographer; courtesy of the Talbot County Historical Society, Easton, Maryland.*

Right: Working boats in an icy marina on Tilghman Island. This photograph was likely taken in the late 1940s. *Laird Wise, photographer; courtesy of the Talbot County Historical Society, Easton, Maryland.*

From January 14 to February 10, the average temperature was more than 9° Fahrenheit below normal, and the minimum temperature for each day during this cold spell was below the freezing point.[307]

The cold detained railroad coal cars for a week, primarily because the coal stockpiles had been frozen solid, making loading and unloading the cars a time-consuming proposition. In the 1940s, anthracite coal was a major home-heating fuel. The Baltimore and Ohio Railroad used a "thawing house" to unfreeze the coal by steam heating it. Nonetheless, an official at the Western Maryland Railroad stated that the unusual cold stretch was adversely affecting every step of the delivery process—from mine to terminal.[308]

Icebreakers fought twelve-foot-thick ice floes near Turkey Point in the upper bay. Oil tankers needed heavy (high-horsepower) tugs to escort them into Baltimore Harbor, and the icebreaker *Annapolis* was called to lead a convoy of barges from Baltimore to Norfolk. Plus, the thick ice was preventing transit through the Chesapeake and Delaware Canal. Ice between six inches and three feet in thickness was measured from Baltimore to the Chesapeake and Delaware Canal.[309]

THE BENTZTOWN BARD

Because the bay is "just around the corner" for many Marylanders and Virginians living east of the Blue Ridge Mountains, it has often been reported on (in all its affairs) by both local and major city newspapers. Articles about the bay were often featured in the *Baltimore Sun*, which has been in circulation since the 1830s. From 1906 to 1948, a *Sun* column titled "Good Morning!" was penned by Folger McKinsey, who went by the moniker "Bentztown Bard (BB)." Able to wax poetic about any subject, he covered his beloved bay no matter the season. For instance, in a column on January 5, 1948, he described the icy Chesapeake Bay in the following manner.[310]

The Winter Bay

Sand bars showing so lone and bare
With the wild winds blowing them dry;
Sea gulls high in the blustering air
Uttering their plaintive cry.
Oyster boats struggling against the gale,
Head winds strong and free,
A leak in the hold and a rent in the sail,
And a tingle of ice on the sea.
From Susquehanna to Pocomoke,
From Chester to Wicomico,
Tankers and freighters with heavy stroke
And tugs with a barge in tow—
Chesapeake winter, ice and snow,
Shore to Shore but a cloud of gloom,
Patuxent, Potomac the Tangier Spray,
The winter bay in its wide blue room
And a foghorn showing the ships their way,
A froth of beauty the whole way along—
Yeah! Come home ships to Patapsco tide,
To the tune of a Canton Hollow song,
To the port of Baltimore's spirit of pride.

In another column from February 27, 1934, it was the bay's boats that captured his attention—in this case, the ferryboat *Smoky Joe*.[311]

The Smoky Joe

When the bay was tight and it meant a fight to break a ship's way down
The Smoky Joe *from the pier at light made her regular trips from town*

She shook her fist in the face of the ice and snorted and churned her way
And she made Love Point and back again—over the Chesapeake Bay,

Captain Woodhall and all his crew were stanch at post of duty;
The captain's word was enough for her, old Smoky Joe, *the beauty*
Twin funnels belching away like hell she crunched her way ahead,
And the ice cakes cracked and roared and shook—and on her way she sped.

Three trips a day when the snow and ice stretched lonely miles and miles.
And she bucked and paused, then backed and filled, and sputtered a thousand styles.
But on she swept like a churning fiend – as over the bay she bore
For three-times-daily her passengers to the good old Eastern Shore.

BB would often write about the watermen and the bay's exquisite bivalve, the oyster, as he did for this January 8, 1948 column.[312]

O Ye Oyster Bed

Of all the beds of now or yore
The bed that I would favor more
Is an oyster bed somewhere not far
Adown the bay, beneath a star
That glimmers over Chesapeake
Its ships with pennants at each peak,
Its foam and mist of changing tides,
Its wind that out of beauty glides
Across far stretches wide and deep,
Give me a bed where oysters sleep,
Grow fat and flavored huge and fine.
A bed, an oyster bed for mine.
A Choptank Bed, a Tangier Bar
Where Maryland's loveliest oysters are.
A mattress of the oyster rock
Where all the little oysters flock
To clutch and stay and feed and dine
On food of Chesapeake, its wine.
Its sea, its salt, its wondrous spell
On flavor as ever swing and swell
The waters chosen by some lot
On faith that God has not forgot.

There are several other "Good Morning!" columns in the *Baltimore Sun* by BB that deal with ice and snow on the Chesapeake Bay; they include the columns from February 23, 1934 (see the cover of this book); March 3, 1947; January 26, 1948; February 6, 1948; and February 18, 1948.[313]

Folger McKinsey was so popular that after illness prevented him from writing his column in 1948, the *Sun*'s readers pleaded to have his columns rerun. And they were for a full year before the Bentztown Bard passed away in 1950.[314]

THE WINTER OF 1955–56

Hard ice formed in the upper Chesapeake Bay in the opening week of 1956 in response to a cold blast of arctic air. This ice, including ice in the Chesapeake and Delaware Canal, solidified after a freighter ran aground, stopping all traffic and thus permitting ice that had been cut to quickly reform. The captain of the *Norwegian Black Heron*, a member of the Association of Maryland Pilots, guided his ship through what he described was the "worst ice he had seen anywhere." It was said that as far south as the Virginia Capes, in the vicinity of Cape Henry, a good many boats were icebound.[315] The ice and cold was relatively short-lived, as warming temperatures brought a quick end to the year's frosty start.

THE WINTER OF 1957–58

It was not until the winter of 1957–58 that the ice on the Chesapeake Bay was as prominent as it had been in the 1930s. By mid-February 1958, the ice was eight inches thick at the mouth of the Potomac, and this ice, stretching from the bay itself to Washington, D.C., was, as a captain of a cargo steamer exclaimed, "no different than the Arctic."[316] It took this steamer several days to stammer up the frozen Potomac to the nation's capital.

THE WINTER OF 1960–61

The winter of 1960–61 was the coldest since 1935–36. By midwinter the cold that gripped the bay had not let up, and heavy ice, even in the main channel of the bay, extended as far south as the mouth of the Patuxent River.[317]

This winter was memorable for its two distinct freezes: the first lasted from mid-December to January 1, and the second lasted from about January 20 to February 20. Following the passage of a cold front on December 13, arctic air spilled into the bay region. In a matter of a day or two, brash and slush ice covered approximately 20 percent of the upper bay. As the cold air remained in place, the ice's thickness increased to five inches north of Baltimore, and coverage was over 80 percent, keeping small crafts in port. Low-powered steamers could push through the ice, but they did so with difficulty. Tributaries on both sides of the bay were encased in ice as far south as Crisfield, near the Maryland–Virginia line on the Eastern Shore. All sailing vessels were confined to their harbors.[318]

By Christmas Day, ice thicknesses of ten to twelve inches were reported in the upper bay. Thus, only icebreakers and vessels with more than one thousand horsepower could navigate the icy waters between Baltimore and the Chesapeake and Delaware Canal. The *Apalachee* and *Chinook* were needed to free several icebound tankers, barges and tugs. Additionally, the ice had separated a number of buoys from their moorings.[319] By January 1, most of this ice had sufficiently thawed, so navigation was unrestricted.

In mid-January, a blast of bitter air dropped temperatures in the bay area to the single digits (Fahrenheit). For twenty-two consecutive days, the temperature remained below normal. By January 20, pancake ice covered about 90 percent of the upper bay. By January 25, nearly 100 percent of the upper bay was iced over, with the ice's thickness measuring more than ten inches in some places. At the month's end, a thickness of thirty-six inches off Tolchester Point in the upper Bay was observed by the crew of the *Apalachee*. Meanwhile, the crew of the *Chinook* confirmed thicknesses of thirty inches in the same area. The calls coming in for assistance were considerable.[320] Ice was then more than just a bother in the mid-bay, and it was affecting transportation in the lower bay as well.

The coast guard cutter *Madrona* was required to keep the waters of the Potomac River, where ice thicknesses of ten inches were noted, open, and the *Barberry* was requested to break ice in the harbors and tributaries of the lower bay. Two other cutters were called to duty; additionally, several icebreaking tugs were in service. On at least one day at the end of January, twelve-icebreaking vessels were plowing through the ice of the bay's waters.

When air temperatures plummeted to the 0° Fahrenheit mark across portions of the mid- and upper bay, the ice became nearly impassable—except by cutters and high-horsepower tugs. Oil tankers were unable to routinely reach ports on the Eastern Shore, so fuel oil was becoming a precious commodity. The communities on Smith and Tangier Islands were yet again isolated by ice. Helicopters were brought in to deliver vital supplies to them until icebreakers could cut a reliable path to the small island harbors.[321] The ice was nearly unbroken all the way from Havre de Grace to the mouth of the Potomac River.

The bay was essentially closed to shipping. Even the main channels of the upper and mid-bay areas were 100 percent ice covered. Oceangoing vessels were able to deliver goods to the Virginia Capes at the southern end of the lower bay, but transit from Philadelphia to Baltimore and Washington, D.C., through the Chesapeake and Delaware Canal was closed. This meant additional time and money were needed to deliver supplies. It is estimated that the ice cost shipping companies $1 million due to delays—a hefty sum in 1961.[322]

It was not until February 9 that a 7,500-ton freighter was able to push through the Chesapeake and Delaware Canal—the canal was completely shut down for a period of fifteen days. By mid-February, a substantial thaw had set in, and after February 20, the entire bay was open to navigation, bringing to a close the winter that had the heaviest ice since 1936.

THE CHESAPEAKE BAY BRIDGE

On the night of February 2, 1961, drivers crossing the Chesapeake Bay Bridge could feel it shudder as slabs of heavy ice were thrust against its supports. It had to be frightening to be in a vehicle over the icy bay, wondering if you would make it to the other side. Later that night, a tug was brought in by the Maryland Port Authority to help break up the ice.

The Chesapeake Bay Bridge spans the bay just north of Annapolis, connecting the Eastern Shore of Maryland to the western shore.[323] This 4.3-mile-long bridge first opened in July 1952.[324] The main shipping channel passes beneath the main span of the bridge, which has a horizontal navigational clearance of 1,500 feet from one support to the next and a vertical navigational clearance of 186 feet from the water surface to the bottom of the roadway.[325] Although engineering studies had been conducted to ensure that the bridge could withstand the pressure of the ice floes, this impressive structure had not yet been tested by a long, icy winter.

After the ice around the pilings was removed, the coast guard set up regular patrols, using the *Cherokee* and *Utina* around the bridge to break up the huge ice floes moving down from the upper bay on ebb currents. The ice's thickness in the main channel of the bay, near the bridge, measured at about six inches on February 6, but the rafted ice was several feet thick.[326]

Ice can behave in some remarkable ways when under pressure. The coast guard cutter *Apalachee* was struggling in two- to three-foot-thick ice while towing a tug off Tolchester Point. When it became completely sealed in, it had to release its tow. Soon, ice pressure caused it to list fifteen degrees to its starboard as ice rafted against its port side, climbing nearly to the deck's level as the anxious crew watched helplessly. As quickly as the ice had ascended and the *Apalachee* heeled, the ice began to fall away. Within perhaps thirty minutes, the cutter had righted itself and was able to continue without further incident. By this time, the ice pressure had eased enough that the tug no longer needed assistance.[327]

THE CHESAPEAKE BAY BRIDGE-TUNNEL

The second major bridge to span the Chesapeake, the Chesapeake Bay Bridge-Tunnel, was erected during the winter of 1960–61. This marvel is partially supported by artificial islands. The roadway itself sits on stilts until it disappears beneath the waves. After opening in April 1964, the 17.6-mile-long combination bridge and tunnel—still considered the world's longest bridge-tunnel complex—linked Virginia's Eastern Shore to the populous Hampton Roads area.[328] Since the construction of the bridge-tunnel was just underway when the bay began to ice over, the icy waters only minimally affected the construction schedule. However, the following year, one of the most significant storms to ever impact the Chesapeake Bay temporarily shut down construction. In early March 1962, a violent nor'easter barreled up the mid-Atlantic coast, bringing a devastating tidal surge, wind gusts in excess of seventy miles per hour, drenching rain and, in the western portions of the bay's watershed, heavy snow.[329] Because this storm, dubbed the "Ash Wednesday Storm," hit late in the season, new ice formation was only a minor concern. Nevertheless, towering waves trashed the construction cranes and barges, burying one of the barges so deep in the sand that it could not be recovered.[330] Understandably, work on the bridge-tunnel was delayed for weeks.

THE WINTER OF 1962–63

A cold December chilled the bay waters, and as Siberian air filtered into the Chesapeake Bay area, ice quickly formed, particularly in the upper bay and its tributaries. Ice between two and five inches thick in the open upper bay slowed some ships and stopped others. So, in late 1962, coast guard cutters were already hard at work. Off the Elk Neck Peninsula, ice was reported to be up to eighteen inches thick in places. Because there was a longshoremen's strike in progress, larger vessels that would normally be able to break through newly forming ice were kept in port. Thus, smaller boats were finding the going more difficult.[331]

The coast guard employed a convoy system that was initiated during the winter of 1961–62, whereby two cutters (the *Chinook* and the *Apalachee*) were utilized to move a convoy of three ships and two tow barges. Another cutter, the *Madrona*, was dispatched from Norfolk to right buoys that had been displaced by strong winds or dragged beneath the ice.[332]

A dock destroyed by ice and tides. This photograph was taken in February 1967. *Charles C. Harris, photographer; courtesy of the Talbot County Historical Society, Easton, Maryland.*

John M. Dennis (Claiborne–Annapolis Ferry) moving through ice. This photograph was taken in 1971. *Charles C. Harris, photographer; courtesy of the Talbot County Historical Society, Easton, Maryland.*

In addition to the years discussed above, during the fifty-seven years between 1920 and 1977, ice on the bay became a significant deterrent to navigation and, to some degree, affected normal fishing (including crabbing and oystering) during the winters of 1922–23, 1933–34, 1967–68, 1969–70 and 1970–71.

15

ICE IN THE BAY

1977

THE WINTER OF 1976–77

Weather during the winter of 1976–77, particularly during the month of January, made headlines for its severity over the eastern two-thirds of the nation—basically all areas east of the Rocky Mountains. Across much of the Upper Midwest and the northern Great Plains, departures from the normal temperatures in January exceeded 10° Fahrenheit. Even greater departures were recorded in the Ohio Valley; Cincinnati, Ohio, observed a departure of -19° Fahrenheit. In Miami, Florida, falling snow was seen for the first time ever, and the temperature in Key West, Florida (located at sea level and less than twenty-five degrees latitude from the equator), dipped below the freezing point. Hard freezes destroyed thousands of acres of Florida's citrus crop and leafy vegetable crops. In the Chesapeake Bay area, it was the coldest winter since the winter of 1917–18.[333]

The atmospheric circulation pattern that generated the brutally cold air had been in place since October 1976, pushing pulse after pulse of arctic air southeastward, through Canada and into the United States. As an Aleutian low deepened off the Pacific coast of North America later in the fall, the upper atmosphere ridge of high pressure over western North America strengthened, as did the trough of low pressure over eastern North America.[334] When strong high-pressure systems (termed arctic blocks) form over the Arctic Ocean, the stage is set for the refrigerated surface air to blast southward, funneling between the upper air western ridge and eastern trough.

By January, with snow cover having been established since October in central Canada, there was little modification of the arctic air as it plunged southward. However, because the upper air flow was coming from the northwest for much of the fall and winter, precipitation was generally below normal. Thus, the winter of 1976–77 was not especially snowy, except in the lee areas of the Great Lakes, where prodigious lake effect snowfalls occurred until the lakes froze over, cutting off their moisture supply.[335]

What was particularly interesting about this pattern was its persistence. Once initiated (in the fall of 1976), it continued unabated through January, not only at the surface, but also through the troposphere and into the lower and middle stratosphere.

The cold air that came was relentless. Almost every weather station east of the Mississippi River ranked the winter of 1976–77 as one of four coldest on record. Some stations in the Ohio Valley and Great Lakes Basin reported below-normal temperatures every day in January 1977. Residents who lived in the wide belt from Iowa to western Pennsylvania and into New York State never saw the thermometer pass the freezing mark for the entire month of January 1977. Never before—since temperatures had first been observed and routinely recorded around the end of the nineteenth century—had such continuously cold air gripped this region. In fact, the daily high and low temperatures in Ohio were lower for many days than they were in Alaska.

By February, the main players in the overall circulation pattern had changed very little, but slight shifts in their positions—a northern displacement in the strongest core of the polar jet stream, for instance—resulted in more moderate temperatures in the eastern United States. The first ten days of February 1977 were still quite cold throughout the Northeast and Mid-Atlantic regions, but because of a welcome warming at the month's end, temperatures in the Mid-Atlantic region were close to normal during the rest of the month.

THE WEATHER IN THE BAY REGION

In January and February 1977, the ice covered the bay as extensively as it had during any year in the nineteenth century, and it certainly rivaled the icy conditions of the winter months of 1918. The epic ice was a direct result of the abnormally cold temperatures that prevailed throughout the bay area from October 1976 to the third week of February 1977. Additionally, August and September 1976 were both relatively chilly months.[336]

The autumn of 1976 was more than 4° Fahrenheit cooler than the long-term normal, as measured at Baltimore-Washington International Airport.[337] In Washington, D.C., at the Washington National Airport, the first frost of the season occurred on October 28, more than a month earlier than the previous fall's first frost and about two weeks earlier than the mean date for the first freeze (32° Fahrenheit).[338] October was also a very wet month—the wettest in thirty-five years.[339]

By November, this cold weather pattern had become firmly established. Below-normal temperatures were observed for twenty-five days in November in the Baltimore and Washington, D.C. area. Contrary to October, November 1976 was one of the driest Novembers on record—only two Novembers were drier in the previous forty years.[340]

Though December 1976 was colder than normal (2.7° Fahrenheit below normal in Baltimore), there was little indication of the bitter cold that would follow at the onset of the new year. During the last ten days of the month, cold air masses surged into the northern plains of the United States and spread southeastward. Like November, December was a dry month, as moisture from the Gulf of Mexico was cut off from the north by a strong northwesterly airflow.[341]

January started off bitterly cold and remained that way. In Baltimore, the temperature departure for the month was -10.5° Fahrenheit. Not since January 1881 had the January temperature failed to reach 50° Fahrenheit. Wilmington, Delaware, and Norfolk, Virginia, experienced their coldest Januarys ever. Perhaps the coldest week of the winter was the last week of January 1977. An extremely cold air mass plunged into the Ohio Valley and then moved on to the Mid-Atlantic region. Blizzard conditions and numbing cold gripped the area from the Great Lakes to the New England and Mid-Atlantic regions. Precipitation was again below normal, but all the precipitation that fell was frozen. Because of the persistent cold, snow remained on the ground for forty consecutive days in many locations in central Maryland.[342]

In response to the cold air, water temperatures in the bay were also well below normal during the fall of 1976 and winter of 1977. From October to December, water temperatures averaged 3° Fahrenheit below normal, with January temperatures measuring 6° Fahrenheit colder than normal. Thus, the bay was primed to freeze solid when blasts of arctic air penetrated the Mid-Atlantic region in early January 1977.

Ice rapidly expanded from north to south, from shallower to deeper water and from protected inlets to the open bay. The ice was confined to the

A Landsat satellite image of ice in the Chesapeake Bay that was acquired on January 15, 1977. *Courtesy of NASA.*

northern tributaries in late December, but by mid-January, it had expanded south of the Chesapeake Bay Bridge and Annapolis. The maximum ice cover was reached in early February, when an estimated seven-eighths, or about 85 percent, of the bay was encased in ice.[343]

Each new incursion of polar air was ushered in on strong northwest or westerly winds. This forced the ice that had formed in the mid-bay to pile up along the Eastern Shore, leaving a portion of the western shore, between the Bay Bridge and the mouth of the Potomac River, free of ice in mid- and late January. Satellite views of the Chesapeake Bay showed patterns of longitudinal cracking and compression fracturing. Subsiding winds in early February allowed ice to reform in the areas that had previously been ice-free.

By late February, temperatures began to moderate, and by early March, with the arrival of unusually warm air, nearly all the bay ice had melted. Even though the average air temperature in the bay area was above normal for February, the first three weeks of the month were quite cold, averaging 2° Fahrenheit below normal in Washington, D.C. However, the last week of the month was spring-like, averaging about 14° Fahrenheit above normal.[344]

Ship passage and navigation were hazardous throughout the entire bay from late January to mid-February and in the upper Bay from late December to late February. Only ships that had steel hulls and a minimum of one-thousand-horsepower engines were permitted in the bay. U.S. Coast Guard cutters and tugs operated by the Maryland Department of Natural Resources (MDNR) were kept busy, clearing shipping lanes and freeing ships that had seized in the ice. Cutters also played an active role in leading convoys into ice-choked harbors, such as Baltimore and Cambridge, and communities that had been completely isolated by the ice, particularly Smith and Tangier Islands. The coast guard cutter *Chinook* answered eighty-seven assist calls in January and February 1977.[345]

An aerial view of a coast guard cutter in the Chesapeake Bay. This photograph was taken in January or February 1977. *Courtesy of the U.S. Coast Guard.*

A coast guard cutter breaking ice in the upper Chesapeake Bay. This photograph was taken in January 1977. *Courtesy of the U.S. Coast Guard.*

A coast guard cutter with a tug in background. This photograph was taken in January 1977. *Courtesy of the U.S. Coast Guard.*

Rafted ice slabs piled along the shore. This photograph was taken in the winter of 1977. *Charles C. Harris, photographer; courtesy of the Talbot County Historical Society, Easton, Maryland.*

The persistent ice and cold water took their toll on fish and marine life, particularly shellfish. In some places in the upper bay, the mortality rate among the bay's aquatic life was as high as 77 percent. Moreover, numerous piers, marinas, lighthouses and docks were damaged by the pressure of crushing ice on flow tides or transported by strong winds.[346]

At the time of the greatest ice cover extent (early February), thicknesses up to twenty-four inches were recorded by the coast guard and MDNR in tributaries entering the northern bay. Ice in the tributaries entering the lower bay measured up to fourteen inches thick. In the open bay, ice in the northern reaches ranged from six to twelve inches thick; while in the open lower bay, thicknesses reached between two and eight inches.[347] In the Wicomico and Nanticoke Rivers on Maryland's southern Eastern Shore, the ice remained a fixture through early March.

SOCIOECONOMIC IMPACTS

By the Christmas and holiday season, ice had already formed near the shore in the upper bay, and the streams and sloughs that enter the upper and mid-bay areas were frozen solid as the new year began. Old-timers who made their living on the bay could not recall a December and January that were so cold—even the icy winter of 1917–18.[348]

By early January, the bay ice was more than conversational, it was becoming a real concern for watermen and anyone who relied on the open water for their livelihood and for the delivery of necessities, such as heating

Big Lou working a little too hard, with its crew (Larry Hopkins and Joe Jones). This photograph was taken in January or February 1977. *Courtesy of the Talbot County Historical Society, Easton, Maryland.*

fuel. Oystering and commercial fishing—and, thus, seafood processing—all but ceased. With the demand up but the supply at rock bottom, oysters were selling for ten dollars a bushel, which was unheard of at the time.[349] As much as 50 percent of bottom blue crabs, 20 percent of oysters and 90 percent of barnacles (crucial to the health of the food chain) perished in the dreadful ice and cold that characterized the bicentennial winter of 1976–77.[350]

President Jimmy Carter declared a state of emergency for many areas along the Eastern Seaboard, and following the lead of President Gerald Ford during the oil embargo of 1974, Carter implored all Americans to turn down their thermostats. For residents on the remote Smith Island, Maryland's governor Marvin Mandel ordered state helicopters to fly in needed goods and supplies. With no way for the few school-aged kids on Smith Island to get to their classes in Crisfield (on the Eastern Shore in Somerset County), teachers sent their assignments by helicopter. The schoolyard of the makeshift school building on the Smith Island also served as the helicopter's landing pad.[351] Any lesson that was being taught during a landing or takeoff was a lesson that needed to be repeated.

With such unusual and constantly cold weather, sensational lead stories on televised news programs and headlines in newspapers were omnipresent during the winter of 1977. In the bay area, newspapers frequently mentioned the icy waters of the Chesapeake—how the cold and ice impacted school closings, power outages, natural gas supplies, marine life and farming (beef and dairy cows and poultry). The following is a selection of newspaper headlines from the *Washington Star* (defunct since 1980) and the *Washington Post* from January 1977.[352]

January 11: Winter Storm Causing Coldest Winter in Decades

January 16: In the Bay: Thaw Only Makes It Worse
Since January 1, two coast guard cutters have run shipping convoys from Baltimore down the bay once per day. Ice sheets in the northern bay are more than a foot thick in places.

January 17: Area Gets No Respite, Bitter Cold Lingers

January 18: Record Cold Cripples Area; Power Cut in Virginia, Schools Shut
Never has there been recorded such a cold January 17 in metropolitan Washington. It was so cold, there was not only a record low temperature -2 at DCA, but a record low maximum +18.

January 19: Bone Chilling Cold Plagues Area, Fires Add to Misery of Areas Numbing Cold Wave
Coast guard vessel leads ships freed from ice yesterday into Baltimore Harbor. 2,570 motorists reported to AAA their cars wouldn't start. Water pipes burst. Virginia's governor Godwin asked President Ford to declare the Chesapeake area a disaster area.

January 24: Ice Cripples Bay Fishing Industry: Tangier, Smith Island Residents Imperiled
First Bay freeze over since 1936.

January 28: Virginia Orders Gas Cutoffs to Firms, Schools in East Area, Lights at the White House Will Go Out Two Hours Early, Swift Action Promised on Gas Crisis Bill

January 30: Carter Sees 4-Day Week as Possibility, Mayor Washington Orders 8-Hour Day, 65 Degrees in All DC Gov't Buildings, Most Baltimore Restuarants Closed as Gas Supply Is Cut Off, All Industrial Gas in MD Reduced to Bare Minimum

January 31: Cold Cripples Eastern Shore Economy
Oystering, key to area industry, brought to standstill. Iceberg, 100 feet long, 40 feet wide, and 20 feet high, appears in the Chesapeake Bay.

Similar headlines continued throughout the first ten days of February. Nonetheless, the thickening expanses of ice enabled residents to indulge in several recreational activities that are typically pursued during wintertime in the northern United States and Canada. Iceboat races were hurriedly organized on some Eastern Shore rivers, including the Miles River at St. Michaels.[353] People with sleds took to the ice; in some cases, the sleds were simply patio chairs. Ice skates, some crudely homemade, were donned by many for once-in-a-lifetime excursions across the bay area's rivers and embayments. The bravehearted slid their way from Chestertown to Cliffs Point and back (a total of nearly seventeen miles).[354] Sandy Point, on the western shore, near the Chesapeake Bay Bridge, and the tidal basin in the nation's capital served as impromptu gathering places for ice skaters on the rare Saturdays or Sundays that the winds were calm and the biting cold had ebbed.

Old beat-up cars were seen doing figure eights on frozen rivers, and go-cart owners saw the bay ice as a new challenge. Lawn tractors served as stand-ins for horses, pulling sleds behind them. A few enterprising watermen were observed tonging from the back of their pickup trucks.[355] Just about every river that enters the upper and mid-bay became a playground for skaters and ice fishermen alike. This also happened, so it seems, during every bitter winter in which big ice formed on the Chesapeake Bay; some claimed to have walked or skated across the bay, from Sandy Point, north of Annapolis, to Kent Island.

There are many remarkable stories about harrowing experiences on the ice that winter as well as silly anecdotes about school-age children and young adults alike being knuckleheads. The following is a sampling of recollections from bay area residents who lived through this phenomenal winter.[356]

I remember the Wicomico River being frozen solid that year. Coast guard cutters had to come up and down the river to break up the ice so oil barges could get through. What a noise the ice made when it was breaking up, an eerie sound, especially during the middle of the night!
—Alice F.

That's the freeze up when I was eleven years old. I almost died. Winds were thirty miles per hour. We skated out such a long way on the bay, and I tried to skate back. I was so cold! I was actually trying to fall asleep. We stopped at Dobbins Island to warm up. Everything was ice. My buddy made it home and finally came to rescue me.
—Lenny T.

That was the year the ocean froze at Ocean City. It was odd standing on the beach and not hearing waves break.
—Susan W.

There were all kinds of waterfowl in the field behind our house. I'm talking about canvasbacks, redheads, blue bills and other diving ducks that never leave the deep water.
—Charles

Being sixteen at that time, all I have are fond memories of that winter. I lived on the Choptank River. Everything was frozen and white. You would step right off the sea wall onto ice, your private ice river! I would wear two coats; the second one a no-sleeved vest. All you had to do was open it up wide and you were off! So fast, you felt as if you were flying. We got so good at this that we learned to use the vest almost as if it were a rudder and could control direction. Of course, the dogs would be trying to keep up with us and were sliding all over the place.
—Maeve F.

I lived in the D.C. area then, and the Potomac had eighteen inches of ice on it. People descended from all over to get to the tidal basin for skating. I skated down as close to the Fourteenth Street Bridge as I could get and as far north as the Key Bridge and crossed over to the Virginia side a few times before stopping to get warm.
—Steve B.

My friend Bobby drove a Volkswagen from Valentine Creek [Severn River] *to the Severn River Bridge and then all the way to the Bay Bridge!*
—Barton J.

I was a young teacher on Smith Island that winter. The elementary school had classes from 9:00 a.m.–3:30 p.m., and high school students came in from 4:00 p.m.–6:00 p.m. as sort of a study hall, thanks to their teachers in Crisfield who sent assignments over by helicopter. The helicopters landed in the schoolyard several times a day bringing supplies for the stores, medicine, et cetera. After about the fifth landing, I was able to get through a lesson without all heads turning toward the windows!
—Barbara T.

The summer of 1976, on the longest day of the year, my husband, Tom, and three friends played one hundred holes of golf in a single day to celebrate the bicentennial. His prize for having the lowest score was a 1962 (I believe) Simca automobile that was painted red, white and blue and donated by the local Ford dealership. By late fall in 1976, that car already was known for constantly breaking down. Tommy sold it to a waterman for one hundred dollars and kept the one-hundred-dollar bill in his wallet for years! The waterman took it out on the ice, cut a hole in order to ice fish…but the car fell thru the ice and sank.
—Jeanne E.

I remember hearing that two boys walked over the ice to Saxis (on Virginia's Eastern Shore)…with only socks on. Later, one of them had to have a foot amputated because of frostbite.
—Martha L.

I was eighteen and dating a guy whose family was from Tangier Island. We took the mail boat over to the island to attend a New Year's Eve party. Long story short, we were stuck there for a week! I sat in the bathroom next to a kerosene heater reading a stack of National Geographic *magazines. After a week, my mother hired a plane to pick us up—I had never flown before and was scared to death! Once in the air, I remember looking down and seeing the coast guard cutters trying to break through to Tangier Island.*
—Terri P.

Near the mid-bay, along the western shore of southern Maryland, at the tip of Calvert County, two men who were thirsty for one of the bay's cold pleasures but without reliable transportation decided to walk to the nearest tavern, which just happened to be in the next county (St. Mary's) on the other side of the wide mouth of the Patuxent River. In other years, their problem would have likely been unresolved, but this year, their thirst and sense of adventure had an obvious solution. Skirting the few openings in the three-inch-thick ice kept them alert but undeterred, and they reached their destination, located seven-eighths of a mile away, in about an hour. They returned the same way they had arrived, perhaps zigging and zagging a bit more. According to locals, this was the first time since the winter of 1936 that anyone had the "courage" to make such a trek. Less than a year after the duo conquered the iced-over river, a new bridge opened over the Patuxent River, making any similar crossings in the future unnecessary, you would think.[357]

The cold was perhaps most mentioned on January 17 and again on January 28. When yet another cold front on January 16 sent air temperatures toward 0° Fahrenheit, automobile mechanics, plumbers and roofers (ice-clogged gutters) were kept busy. Bursting pipes were huge problems, as were car engines that were protesting the cold. Balky furnaces were running seemingly nonstop. At Washington National Airport, the low temperature fell to -2° Fahrenheit, the second coldest reading since 1940, when the thermometer was located on the Washington Mall (near the Smithsonian Museums). Its current location on the shore of the Potomac River is recognized as being warmer than the in-town site. At Dulles International Airport, approximately thirty miles west of Washington, D.C., January 17 was the third of four consecutive days that the minimum temperature plunged below the 0° Fahrenheit degree mark.[358]

On January 28, yet more polar air raced south into the Ohio Valley. The month's highest temperature in the bay area had occurred just the day before, but later that day, the month's strongest wind gusts and the bitter air that accompanied them quickly overtook the relative warmth. Riding the gust front were snow squalls that reduced visibility to less than one-tenth of a mile. At the day's end, temperatures across the bay area were near or below 0° Fahrenheit. The temperature range from the afternoon of January 27 to the morning of January 28 was thought to be unprecedented—some locations experienced a drop of almost 50° Fahrenheit in sixteen hours.[359]

This fresh surge of cold air further diminished the withering fuel supplies, especially natural gas. Some jurisdictions ordered government buildings to

A food delivery vehicle stuck in ice on the frozen Patuxent River. This photograph was taken in January 1977. *Courtesy of the Calvert Marine Museum.*

set temperatures no higher than 65° Fahrenheit during the day and 55° Fahrenheit during the night. The counties in Maryland and Virginia that bordered the Chesapeake Bay were all declared disaster areas. Barges that had been able to extricate themselves from the bay's ice during the relatively warmer weather of January 27 were locked in again by the cold blast that arrived later that night. For the second time since the middle of January, pipes broke, car engines would not turn over and furnaces were reluctant to kick on, keeping servicemen fully occupied.[360] In St. Mary's County (in southern Maryland), watermen estimated that the ice along shore was eight to ten inches thick.[361]

At the end of the month, an odd apparition was spotted by a coast guardsman off the mouth of the Chester River: a massive pile of ice that was twenty feet tall, forty feet thick and about one hundred feet long. Perhaps built as strong westward winds pushed ice against the Eastern Shore, heaping new ice on top of already existing ice rafts, it loomed over the river's entrance and appeared like an iceberg in the Arctic Ocean. In the unrelenting cold—indeed, the arctic air of January 1977—it seemed like this huge cube would stay frozen until summer. Alas, it melted away by early March, as did the rest of the bay's ice. It was an epic ice year in the Chesapeake Bay, but it was not so epic as to withstand the sun's slow but sure trek northward.

NATIONALLY: THE WINTER OF 1976–77
VERSUS THE WINTER OF 1917–18

The climatology of the winters of 1917–18 and 1976–77 was remarkably similar. Both winters had anomalously chilly autumns. The cold deepened as autumn transitioned to winter and persisted, with little interruption, into mid-February. In the Ohio Valley, maximum temperature departures approached 10° Fahrenheit. Departures were slightly greater during the winter of 1917–18 across the northern tier of the United States, from the Dakotas to New England, and in the Mid-Atlantic region; whereas during the winter of 1976–77, the cold penetrated farther south. East of the ninetieth meridian (a north-to-south line from approximately New Orleans, Louisiana, to Madison, Wisconsin), the winter of 1976–77 was the coldest of the twentieth century. From the Rocky Mountains eastward, the winter of 1917–18 was fractionally colder.[362]

In both years, January, not surprisingly, brought the coldest winter weather. In several locations in the Mid-Atlantic region, including New York City and Washington, D.C., January 1918 was the coldest January ever recorded. But in Philadelphia, Pennsylvania; Wilmington, Delaware; Baltimore, Maryland; and Lynchburg and Richmond, Virginia, January 1977 holds the distinction of the coldest January on record.

There were no upper-air weather charts available in the early twentieth century, so a rigorous comparison between the two winters is not possible. Regardless, it is likely that the surface weather and the upper-air circulation from October to February in both these years were very similar.

16

ICE IN THE BAY

Late 1900s

THE WINTER OF 1977–78

The winters in the late 1970s through the early 1980s were generally quite cold in the eastern United States, and as a result, the Chesapeake Bay experienced greater than normal icing conditions during this period.

The winter of 1977–78 marked only the third time in the twentieth century that back-to-back abnormally cold winters were observed in the Chesapeake Bay area. The period between December 1977 and February 1978 was actually colder than it had been over the same period just one year before.[363] The bay was not as icy, however, since the autumn temperatures during the fall of 1977 were not nearly as cold as the temperatures experienced during the fall of 1976.[364] And although January 1978 was colder than normal, it did not match the record-breaking cold of the previous January.[365] Still, the air temperature in Baltimore never exceeded 50° Fahrenheit from January 1 to February 25, and snow remained on the ground continuously on north-facing slopes for sixty days. This was perhaps the longest period of consecutive snow cover since the winter of 1917–18.[366]

By mid-February 1978, the coast guard reported that only minor floes had formed south of the Bay Bridge, but the ice cover was solid in the upper bay and its northern tributaries. This was also the case the year before, with strong prevailing winds from the northwest dislodging shore ice from the bay's western shore; though, it wasn't compacted to the same degree against the Eastern Shore then as it was in January and February 1977.[367]

The maximum ice coverage during the winter of 1977–78 occurred in mid-February, about a week later than it had in 1976–77; approximately

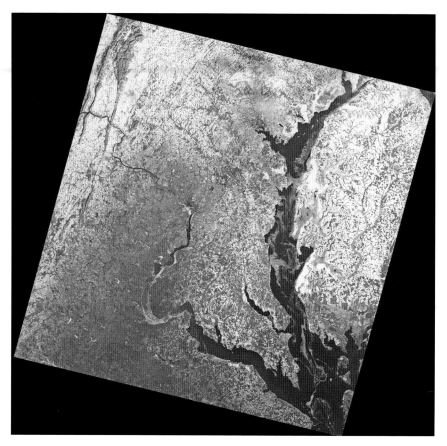

A Landsat satellite image of ice in the Chesapeake Bay that was acquired on February 15, 1978. *Courtesy of NASA.*

30 percent of the bay was frozen, as determined by Landsat satellite observations.[368] Because the cold this winter was so persistent, northern portions of the bay remained ice-covered as late as mid-March. The author of this book recalls walking with a friend across a section of the frozen Tridelphia Reservoir (on the upper Patuxent River) on March 7, 1978. The ice on the reservoir was at least six inches thick.

Navigation was hindered by the ice during January and February, but most shipping channels had only limited ice coverage, allowing transit without restrictions on horsepower. Furthermore, the damage done to the marine life and shellfish populations was minimal during the winter of 1977–78.[369] Oystermen employing tongs were able to harvest bivalves with only occasional ice-related interruptions.

THE WINTER OF 1978–79

The winter of 1978–79 was, again, much colder than normal—the third consecutive icy winter of the late 1970s.[370] Ice cover was more extensive this year than it had been in 1977–78, but it was not nearly as severe as it was during the winter of 1976–77. Temperatures is the fall of 1978 were above normal; however, by January 1979, cold air was forced south from Canada and remained in place until late February.[371] In Baltimore, from February 9 to February 18, the average temperature was 20° Fahrenheit below normal, and for the month, the average temperature was more than 9° Fahrenheit below normal. At many locales in the bay area, for more than half a dozen days, the low temperature dropped below 0° Fahrenheit.[372] In fact, February 1979 was not only the coldest February of the twentieth century in the Chesapeake Bay area, but it was also the snowiest and wettest.

During a majority of February, a strong, quasistationary trough was positioned over eastern North America. This trough maintained a vigorous stream of air from north-central Canada into the United States until the last week of the month. At the surface, a high-pressure area stretched from northeastern Siberia, through Canada and into the United States, permitting pulses of arctic air to penetrate the Mid-Atlantic region.

The climax of this winter came in the form of a prodigious snowstorm on February 18 and 19 (Presidents' Day Storm), with accumulations of over twenty inches of snow measured in many areas around the bay.[373]

The ice cover reached its maximum extent on February 20, when approximately 60 percent of the bay was jammed with ice. Because of cloud cover during the times of satellite overpasses in February 1979, this value is based on coast guard records rather than satellite observations. Note that the maximum ice extent this season occurred later than the previous two winters, about a week later than in 1978 and two weeks later than in 1977.

The coast guard reported that shipping was brought to nearly a halt for about two weeks in February 1979; this compares to about five weeks in February 1977. As in the winter of 1976–77, the large volume of ice necessitated imposing limitations on shipping. All shipping vessels were required to be part of a coast guard convoy, regardless of their cargo, and all vessels were required to have steel hulls and a minimum one-thousand-horsepower engine.

Quickly moving heating fuel to where it is needed most is critical during bitter cold winters. In February 1979, part of a liquefied natural gas pier

A Landsat satellite image of ice in the Chesapeake Bay that was acquired on February 10, 1979. *Courtesy of NASA.*

collapsed after ice compromised concrete pilings at Cove Point, located near the mid-Bay. Because of the damage, tankers were unable to use the pier's north loading berth, thus delaying fuel shipments.[374]

Since the ice was not as thick or as extensive in 1979 as it was in 1977, only minor damage to marine life was observed.[375]

Weather Records in Baltimore (BWI Airport Station) Set During the Winter of 1978–79

January
7.84 inches of precipitation, wettest ever in Baltimore.

February
7.16 inches of precipitation, wettest ever in Baltimore.
33.10 inches of snowfall, snowiest month in the twentieth century in Baltimore.
20.0 inches of snowfall on February 18–19, most ever recorded in a twenty-four-hour period in the twentieth century in Baltimore.
24 inches total snow depth on February 19, second most recorded in the twentieth century in Baltimore.
-3° Fahrenheit on February 10, lowest temperature recorded for any February in the twentieth century in Baltimore.
Average February temperature of 25.8° F, lowest recorded for any February in Baltimore and fifth coldest month ever.

October
October 10, earliest snow accumulation in the twentieth century in Baltimore.

Annual
58.98 inches precipitation, most precipitation in the twentieth century in Baltimore.

NATIONALLY: THE THREE COLD WINTERS OF 1977–79

Based on temperature data from the National Climatic Data Center in Asheville, North Carolina, the three cold winters between 1977 and 1979 were unparalleled nationally. In the eastern United States, where some temperature records go back to the late eighteenth century, January 1977 was possibly the coldest month in two hundred years.[376]

In January 1979, temperatures nationwide were even colder than in January 1977; 98 percent of the contiguous United States experienced below-normal temperatures. Truth be told, the average temperature this month, for the entire nation, was a stunning 22.8° Fahrenheit, colder than any other month on record.[377]

These were the three coldest consecutive winters ever recorded. Furthermore, the unusual precipitation patterns, including heavy snowfall east of the Mississippi and severe drought in the western states, were thought to be the most extreme since the early 1900s.[378]

Meteorologists and climatologists have acknowledged the oddity of this streak. Sunspot numbers and volcanic eruptions were looked at as possible reasons for the three-year period of unprecedented winter cold and chaotic weather patterns. Were we headed into a new Little Ice Age?

ICEBOAT RACING

Iceboats have been around for hundreds of years. They were probably first raced in the mid-nineteenth century. On open ice expanses, winds can propel the boats to speeds in excess of seventy miles per hour. The ice must be reliably solid (several inches thick) over a course that is at least one mile in length. Moreover, the ice must be free of any pressure ridges or cracks, and there should be no snow on top of the ice. Such conditions are infrequently met in the Chesapeake Bay, thus iceboat racing on the bay and its wide-mouthed rivers is generally limited to the coldest winters when snowfall is below normal.

The cold winters of the 1960s and 1970s produced a surge in iceboat racing on the bay; 1969–70 and 1976–77 were banner years for this wintertime sport.[379]

Iceboats are raced in several different classes that depend on the boat's overall length. The popular DN (stands for *Detroit News*) class is for boats that are twelve feet in length and carry sixty-seven square feet of sail.[380] Boats that are larger than this are manned by two sailors. In addition to the sail, iceboats have three runners and a tiller that is used to steer the front runner. The runners are critical in how fast boats travels. One is placed directly under the bow, and one is placed on each end of the planks, crossing under the "cockpit." It is important to make sure the runners are all parallel. Of course, the smoother the runner, the faster the boat will move. So, boaters have their own formulas for sanding, filing and greasing their runners to ensure minimum friction with the ice's surface.

These boats are actually easier to sail on ice than on water, since there is less resistance offered by smooth ice. To pick up the wind, one of the sailors must lie flat on the boat, holding the tiller, and their teammate has to give them a running push. It may take several minutes to reach top speeds. To stop the boat, one must simply steer it directly into the wind.[381] The winds should not be too strong, however. Since a boat may accelerate to a speed three times faster than the wind speed, turning becomes near impossible if gusts exceed forty miles per hour.

Iceboats on the Eastern Shore of Maryland. *Courtesy of the Historical Society of Cecil County.*

Beautiful ice conditions on the Chesapeake in the winter of 1977 lured the North American Ice Boat Championship to the Miles River (Miles River Yacht Club, near St. Michaels). The races were held in early February 1977.[382] Because ice conditions cannot be forecast months in advance, the venue and dates for the championship were not determined until the ice began to form. Competitors obviously need to be flexible. In the winter months of 1977, ice formed all along the northeast and mid-Atlantic coasts, as well as on the Great Lakes, but major snowstorms and blizzards often resulted in snow-covered ice, undesirable for iceboat racing. The Chesapeake Bay was one of the few areas with both solid ice and minimal snow cover. Thus, for the first time ever, championship iceboat racing took place on the bay.

Approximately one hundred boats entered the competition, with fifty-five qualifying for the championship finals. On clean ice that was some eight to ten inches thick, twenty- to thirty-mile-per-hour winds accelerated the boats to sixty miles per hour. However, newly formed pressure ridges, which can be several inches high, compromised top speeds.[383]

The location of the racecourse was changed to fit the changing ice conditions. Fortunately, the Miles River's broad mouth allowed for new

Iceboats and onlookers before the races on the Eastern Shore of Maryland. This photograph was taken in 1977. *Courtesy of Howard Freedlander, photographer.*

courses to be laid out. Pressure ridges are the bane of iceboat racing. Ridges can open in the time between one race ending and another beginning. Several racers were injured and their boats damaged when ridges suddenly appeared in the qualifying heats. A racing official estimated that 20 percent of the one hundred boats were damaged by these ridges.[384]

Ideally, the races are conducted before noon. Once the sun is high overhead and the ice begins to warm, old cracks are more apt to reopen. Saltwater ice is inherently weak compared to freshwater ice, and once the weather warms, the ice on the bay's estuaries can quickly "rot." With hundreds of spectators on the ice watching the final race of the championship, a Michigan boat claimed the title.[385] Fortunately, the final racing series was unmarred by ridges or leads, allowing for a great day of racing.

THE WINTER OF 1980–81

For the fourth time in five years, the winter of 1980–81 was anomalously cold. From about mid-December to mid-January, frigid air poured into the Mid-Atlantic region.[386] Temperatures below 0° Fahrenheit were not uncommon—apart from in the urban heat islands—during this period. The temperature regime during the winter of 1980–81 was similar to the conditions experienced in 1976–77; in both years, the fall weather was colder than normal, January was extremely cold and February was much more moderate.

By mid-January, much of the bay, to the mouth of the Potomac, was ice-covered. The Potomac River itself and nearly all the tributaries entering the mid- and upper bay were choked with ice. Through much of January, clouds again prevented an accurate satellite estimate of the maximum ice extent, but based on tug reports and satellite views from earlier in the month, at the time of the maximum ice extent, around January 20, perhaps 50 percent of the bay was ice-covered. During this winter, the ice melted faster than it had during the winters of the late 1970s. For the first two weeks of January, all shipping vessels north of the Chesapeake Bay Bridge were required to be in coast guard convoys.[387] Additionally, north of the mouth of the Choptank River, it was mandated by the coast guard that ships had to have steel hulls with a minimum 1,000-horsepower engine. However, in the northern reaches of the upper bay, where some ice floes were four feet thick, vessels were required to have at least 2,500 shaft horsepower.[388]

This was another hard winter for watermen. When working on the ice, getting in a jam can occur in an instant. A lot can go wrong, but more often than not, the tide is involved, resulting in an oysterman's boat getting stuck in ice that quickly forms around it. This is what happened to an oysterman off Kent Island one morning. According to the *Baltimore Sun*, the oysterman's boat was sealed in by ice when the tide switched on him, forcing him to do whatever he could to keep from freezing to death in temperatures that were in the single digits, with wind chills below 0° Fahrenheit. When it was realized he was missing, the coast guard and state marine police were notified, though a coast guard cutter was not nearby at the time, and other boats in his proximity were iced in port. After spending more than twelve hours on the ice by himself, he was finally rescued by a police helicopter.[389] This third-generation waterman had been an oysterman all his life. Typical of all of these rugged souls, he worked in the steam heat and frigid cold. His income lay at the bottom of the bay, and he intended to work his trade whenever possible. After being interviewed by the *Sun*, he stated that he planned to go back on the ice the very next day.[390] Of course, he first had to figure out how to retrieve his icebound boat.[391]

Marine life and shellfish were not seriously harmed by the ice during the winter of 1980–81.[392]

THE WINTER OF 1982 AND THE TRAGEDY OF *AIR FLORIDA* FLIGHT 90

The following winter, 1981–82, was even icier—and the fifth icy winter of the last six. Maryland's governor Harry Hughes asked President Ronald

Reagan to declare that the Chesapeake Bay was in an economic disaster due to severe icing. The ice cost Maryland fishermen about $3 million during the month of January. This amount was chiefly used to pay the unemployment benefits of six thousand watermen who were unable to fish the bay's waters. Even with icebreaking operations, solid ice in the northern and mid-bay areas prevented most watermen from working during the first three weeks of the new year.[393]

In early January, temperatures plummeted to the 0° Fahrenheit mark in the Baltimore suburbs during an incursion of arctic air referred to as the "Siberian Express."[394] The coast guard brought in its newest icebreaker, the 140-foot *Morro Bay*, to help cut the ice, which, by mid-January, was already two feet thick in isolated stretches of the upper bay.[395]

The most notable event of the winter of 1981–82 occurred during a snowstorm on January 13: the crash of *Air Florida* Flight 90, which fell into the icy Potomac River less than a minute after it took off from Washington National Airport. A total of seventy-eight people lost their lives—seventy-three in the plane, four in vehicles that were struck as the plane hit the Fourteenth Street Bridge and one who drowned in the Potomac River.

Although the Boeing 737-222 aircraft had been de-iced just after leaving its gate, snow began to fall in earnest during what would be the season's biggest snowstorm. Because of the decreasing visibility and need to make sure runways were cleared of snow, the airport was temporarily closed as flight 90 waited on the runway. During the forty-five-minute interval between the time the plane was de-iced and the time it was ready for takeoff, snow and ice began accumulating on the surfaces of the plane's wings and tail.[396]

After the pilot decided not to return for another de-icing session and failed to activate the plane's own de-icing system, a substantial amount of ice coated the wings, compromising the planes lift. So, as flight 90 headed down the runway, the stage was set for one of the greatest disasters on the Chesapeake's many waterways—it was certainly the worst in the twentieth century.[397] Due to the additional weight of the ice and snow, as well as the plane's loss of lift, the aircraft took too long to clear the runway and could not achieve sufficient altitude to remain aloft. Within thirty seconds of takeoff, it smacked the Fourteenth Street Bridge (connecting Arlington, Virginia, to Washington, D.C.), which was jammed with commuters who had left their offices early to escape the quickly accumulating snow.[398]

Moments after the plane plunged into the ice-caked Potomac, several passengers who had survived the crash were foundering in the icy water. A

Assisting with the clean-up of the crash of *Air Florida* Flight 90. This photograph was taken in January 1982. *Courtesy of the Associated Press News.*

police helicopter that promptly arrived on the scene dropped lifelines to the passengers who were still in the water. One passenger, Arland Williams Jr., made sure everyone had one of these lines, but sadly, he perished before he could be rescued.[399]

A bystander, Lenny Skutnik, after realizing that a flight attendant was floundering in the water, jumped in to save her. For their heroic efforts that day, both Williams and Skutnik—and another bystander, Roger Olian— were awarded the Coast Guard Gold Lifesaving Medal. Skutnik was also honored at President Reagan's State of the Union Address later that month. The Fourteenth Street Bridge has been renamed the Arland D. Williams Jr. Memorial Bridge.[400]

The City of Washington, D.C., did not own an icebreaker, but a recently purchased fireboat, the *John H. Glenn Jr.*, was able to contribute to the rescue and clean-up efforts. Because the coast guard had a dock in Alexandria on the Virginia side of the Potomac River, the cutter *Capstan* was able to quickly respond. The U.S. Army Corps of Engineers and the U.S. Navy also did whatever was asked of them to help.

THE WINTER OF 1993–94

The winter of 1993–94 was the sixteenth coldest in Maryland since the turn of the twentieth century, and the month of January was the sixth coldest during this period. In fact, January 19, 1994, was possibly the coldest day in Baltimore since records were first kept in 1871: the high was just 5° Fahrenheit, while the low dropped to -5° Fahrenheit. However, ice storms, not snowstorms, were the hallmarks of this winter. Rock-hard ice made traversing driveways and parking lots a nightmare. Some schools were closed for more than two weeks during this winter, and the area airports were shut down for multiple days due to this icy weather.[401] Rivers froze, as did the upper bay and portions of the mid-bay. Tugs and even coast guard cutters were once again called to duty to keep channels open for shipping.

Buoy tenders and tugs were breaking ice and escorting convoys as far south as Tangier Island in the lower bay. On the Eastern Shore of Maryland, a path was cleared for barges carrying thirty-five thousand gallons of home-heating oil up the Wicomico River to Salisbury, which was in desperate need of this fuel. Coast guard cutters were required to open the Chesapeake and Delaware Canal, as well as the lower Potomac River, the Anacostia River in Washington, D.C., and the lower James River in Virginia.[402]

SUMMARY FOR THE 1900s

On at least a dozen occasions during the twentieth century (1901–02, 1903–04, 1904–05, 1916–17, 1917–18, 1935–36, 1960–61, 1962–63, 1976–77, 1978–79, 1980–81 and 1981–82), ice in the bay was extensive, covering approximately 50 percent or more of the bay's surface for at least a two-week period—thus acutely impacting navigation, shipping and fishing.

As was mentioned earlier, in the two most extreme winters, 1917–18 and 1976–77, the ice coverage was of such consequence that it impacted nearly the entire bay for four weeks or more. Not only was normal shipping restricted, but also many towns located on tributaries of the bay were sealed in ice for six consecutive weeks or longer. Ice stretched unbroken all the way from the mouth of the Susquehanna River to well into the lower Bay, covering more than 75 percent of the bay's waters. Furthermore, shellfish suffered high mortality rates, over 50 percent in the upper bay.

The following tables show air temperature and water temperature, respectively, for Baltimore, Maryland, focusing on the bay's two most extreme winters of the twentieth century (1917–18 and 1976–77). The January air temperatures for these two months was -9.2° Fahrenheit below normal and -10.4° Fahrenheit below normal, respectively. No other January since 1900 has been more than -6.0° Fahrenheit below normal. Moreover, the air temperatures were below normal for each month from October to January, averaging 5.8° Fahrenheit below normal for the four months in 1917–18 and 5.9° Fahrenheit below normal for the same months in 1976–77. Water temperatures were also well below normal for the October-to-January period in both of these unforgiving winters.

AVERAGE MONTHLY AIR TEMPERATURE AND DEPARTURES FROM NORMAL (IN BALTIMORE) FOR YEARS WITH SUBSTANTIAL ICE
(Temperature recorded in degrees Fahrenheit)

	Oct.	Nov.	Dec.	Jan.	Feb.	fall–winter (five-month average)
Average temp.	57.1	46.0	36.3	33.4	35.4	
1875–76	-1.9	-1.1	+2.5	-4.0	**-7.0**	11.5/5 -2.3
1880–81	-0.5	**-5.1**	**-5.2**	-3.8	-0.7	15.3/5 -3.1
1892–93	-1.4	**-4.2**	-2.9	**-9.9**	-1.0	18.4/5 -3.7
1894–95	+0.9	**-5.2**	+2.5	-1.6	**-8.7**	12.1/5 -2.4
1901–02	+0.6	**-4.7**	-1.1	-1.3	**-5.4**	11.1/5 -2.2
1903–04	+2.3	-3.3	-3.7	**-5.4**	**-7.2**	17.3/5 -3.5
1904–05	-2.3	-2.7	**-5.1**	-2.1	**-8.5**	29.3/5 **-4.1**
1917–18	**-4.5**	-1.4	**-7.9**	**-9.2**	-1.2	27/5 **-5.4**
1935–36	+1.4	+4.4	-3.5	-2.6	**-5.7**	6/5 -1.2
1960–61	-0.5	+0.9	**-7.9**	**-5.8**	+1.6	10.7/5 -2.1

	Oct.	Nov.	Dec.	Jan.	Feb.	fall–winter (five-month average)
1962–63	+0.6	**-4.5**	**-5.4**	**-4.6**	**-7.6**	21.5/5 **-4.3**
1976–77	**-4.5**	**-5.2**	-3.7	**-10.5**	+1.7	22.2/5 **-4.4**
1977–78	-1.4	+3.1	+0.3	-4.2	**-7.5**	9.7/5 -1.9
1978–79	-1.3	+2.1	+4.9	-0.3	**-9.2**	3.8/5 -0.8
1980–81	-0.8	-2.3	-1.2	**-5.0**	**-4.3**	13.6/5 -2.7
1981–82	-2.8	-0.3	-2.2	**-7.4**	0.0	12.7/5 -2.5
2014–15	+2.1	-3.1	+3.2	-2.1	**-10.5**	11.5/5 -2.3
2017–18	+3.5	-0.3	-1.2			

The numbers in bold indicate one standard deviation (below normal).
The temperature data was taken from www.weather.gov and was collected in
Baltimore, Maryland (official weather station).

AVERAGE MONTHLY WATER TEMPERATURES AND DEPARTURES FROM NORMAL (IN BALTIMORE) FOR SELECTED YEARS
(Temperature recorded in degrees Fahrenheit)

	Oct.	Nov.	Dec.	Jan.	Feb.	fall–winter (five-month average)
Average temp.	64.6	54.2	43.1	37.6	43.0	
1917–18	-4.9	-5.5	-5.9	-5.8	-3.8	26.9/5 **-5.4**
1935–36	-0.7	+2.3	-2.1	-3.3	**-4.7**	7.2/5 -1.4
1960–61	+2.2	+0.2	-1.4	-2.8	-1.0	2.8/5 -0.6
1962–63	+1.5	-2.6	-1.6	-3.4	-4.1	10.2/5 -2.0
1976–77	-2.1	**-6.2**	**-4.6**	**-6.0**	**-4.1**	24/5 **-4.8**
1977–78	-3.0	+0.1	-2.4	-2.1	-3.2	10.6/5 -2.1
1978–79	-2.0	+1.2	+2.7	-1.1	-4.0	3.2/5 -0.6
1980–81						

	Oct.	Nov.	Dec.	Jan.	Feb.	fall–winter (five-month average)
1981–82						
2014–15	+5.4	+3.8	+0.4	+0.9	**-9.5**	1.5/5 +0.3
2017–18	+5.9	+3.8	+1.9	-2.6		

There is no data available for the years prior to 1914. The numbers in bold indicate departures below 4° Fahrenheit.
The data for 1980–81 and 1981–82 is unavailable.
This data is from Coast and Geodetic Survey and was recorded one foot (.3 meters) below the surface.

17

WAYS OF THE WATERMEN

Older watermen today consider the brutal winter of 1976–77 the baseline in their memory banks to compare all other winters against. Despite the hostile working conditions they faced when the bay's waters were icy, watermen found ways to get out on the bay. They dressed in layers and shrugged off the cold as best they could. Realizing that iced-over bays and rivers limit the supply of shellfish, watermen knew that demand would go up, along with the price per bushel at market. It was time to go to work.

In icy waters, skipjacks could work through thin ice but would get wedged in when the ice was thick (more than about two inches in thickness). Heavier boats (boats with engines) could ride up on the ice and then break through, but these boats and others with copper sheeting on their hulls were ineffective in breaking through thick, hard ice. Still, when the ice was sufficiently thick, vehicles of all kinds were utilized to harvest oysters and clams. Sometimes, oystermen would just walk out onto the ice, whack out a hole and use tongs to pull up the goods.

But working as part of a team was much safer than going out alone or with one or two friends. In years like 1977, watermen who were working near St. Michaels would use multiple boats, pushing each other to break through the ice until they reached the oyster grounds. They would try to use the same track each day. But if the previous day's path refroze overnight, it was sometimes actually easier to chart a new course through the ice cover. A few particularly assiduous watermen never lost a day's work that winter.

When ice fishing, iceboating or just walking along a frozen shore, as the ice naturally shifts, sharp retorts can be quite jolting, making one hesitate before taking another step or throwing in another line. Watermen know that when you are worried about the ice, it is time to head to shore.

Some watermen recall pulling up oysters and clams from old cars and pickup trucks when their boats were not up to the job. They would drive out onto the ice, cut out a large hole and drop a dredge into the water. Two vehicles would work in tandem, moving along a line that had been sliced through the ice cover until they reached a hole cut into the end of the line. There, the dredge would be removed, unloaded and dropped back into the water for the return trip. These larger holes were often kept open by geese and other waterfowl. When softshell clams were brought up to the surface, every effort was made to keep them from freezing; this is not an easy trick when air temperatures were well below freezing. They wanted to keep them from freezing because a change in consistency could result in a change in texture and taste.

In late January 1977, strong northwest and western winds forced ice from the western shore of the bay up against the Eastern Shore. When this happened, watermen would stage their boats out of places such as Deale and Solomons Island on the western Shore. Substantial catches were hauled up by gill-netters, and they fished in the ice-free waters until the winds subsided and the bay water refroze.[403]

Even with only a modest layer of snow covering the ice (six inches or so), it is too heavy for most working boats to break through. During the winter of 1976–77, as mentioned earlier there were no major snowstorms that impacted the bay area. However, this was not the case during the winter of 1978–79. The Presidents' Day Storm in 1979 was the largest snowstorm in the mid- and upper bay since the Knickerbocker Storm of 1922. Snowfall totals from this nor'easter measured twenty to twenty-two inches along the western shore, north of Annapolis, and the total snowfall that February eclipsed three feet. When more than one foot of snow covers the ice, all but the largest fractures and cracks are concealed from view, making the bay and its ice-covered rivers even more dangerous for the watermen.[404]

Watermen of today still recall the wintertime tragedies from years ago, when a lot of good men were lost. In February 1979, one of the coldest Februarys of the twentieth century, one boat captain and his party of five, all related to one another, were fishing off Tilghman Island. Because fishing is often best when the weather is worst, even on a miserable midwinter's day, if the ice hadn't sealed, boats went in.

After a day of fishing without incident, cold northwestern winds pushed through that evening as the captain was pulling up his nets. Ice began to form near his fifty-foot boat. It seems that the stern was facing the wind, and at least one wave washed over the deck, shutting down its motor. Other waves did the same. With their boat taking on water, the captain and crew were likely bailing with buckets. But the big fishing boat was quickly swamped; the icy cold water swallowed it up. All on board were lost.

Being a waterman or oystering was and is a tough job. It was a more lucrative job one hundred years ago than it is today, but then as now, the cold and ice, long hours, time away from home and up-and-down wages quickly winnowed the proud watermen from the wannabes.

Most watermen of the Chesapeake, or "sho'men," live on the Eastern Shore or on the bay's islands. Though the Delmarva Peninsula is now more accessible, since the Bay Bridge and bridge-tunnel were built, older residents, particularly the watermen, are still known for their provincialism. They are independent, self-sufficient and have their own way of saying things. If they are not busy, many will gladly share a yarn or two with fellow watermen and strangers alike.[405]

For first-time visitors to the Eastern Shore, interpreting what an oysterman is talking about can be challenging. For example, "That's roight, we lose two, three days a week because it's no breeze, not countin' the times when the bay's froze up,"[406] and, "Going down the bay to plant cultch to catch spat" is interpreted as putting oyster shells (called cultch) on the bottom of the bay to provide a place for the infant oysters (spats) to take hold.[407]

On Smith (Maryland) and Tangier (Virginia) Islands, until the last decade or so of the twentieth century, nearly every working man was a waterman. The men wear weathered faces from years of being out on the bay's waters. Visiting these islands is like stepping back into old England and Ireland—dialects are even harder to understand here than elsewhere in the bay.[408] Before about 1950, it was not unusual to hear of islanders who had died on the island where they were born without ever leaving the environs of the Chesapeake Bay.

A century ago, the islanders could get by when frozen-in—oysters were still plentiful enough so that they could be tonged through the ice. Now, however, fuel and at least some supplies must be brought in from Crisfield, Maryland. So, if a big freeze occurs, help is needed, as the islands' inhabitants are shut off from the mainland. Whenever the ice is thick, icebreakers will pay a visit.

Oystermen didn't take classes to learn that few oysters are brought up in a southeaster or how to read the tides. Their primary learning institutions were the school of hard knocks and the oral history of their predecessors. Whether one's objective is to make the bay cleaner or restore its fishing and oystering, the knowledge of the people working the waters of the Chesapeake should not be neglected.[409]

Expressions learned from years on the water, such as "snow pushes fish toward the bottom, where the nets are" were undeniably useful to watermen.[410] Day-to-day weather on the Chesapeake and season-to-season changes were full of many surprises, but the seasons came in and moved out without fail. Adages like "no winter lasts forever; no spring skips its turn" had true meaning to the watermen.[411]

Life as a waterman on the Chesapeake Bay has not changed dramatically over the centuries.[412] Framed by the vagaries of the weather and the waves, cycles of abundance and shortage and boats crafted with skill and care, watermen have been almost as much a part of the bay as the water that flows through it.

THE WATERMEN'S BOATS

Bugeyes, skipjacks, porgies, sloops, schooners, clippers, deadrises, canoes and skiffs could all have been found in the bay's waters one hundred years ago. Skipjacks, sloops, bugeyes and schooners were primarily used for oystering; the former two are single-masted, and the latter two are double-masted. Around 150 years ago, two thousand of these boats were busy catching oysters. Now, they are a rare sight on the bay.

Skipjacks and other boats in an icy harbor on Tilghman Island. This photograph was likely taken in the late 1970s. *Courtesy of the Talbot County Historical Society, Easton, Maryland.*

Bugeyes were first built in the early 1800s. Predecessors to the nimbler skipjacks, typical bugeyes were about fifty-five feet long. Most had two masts, but some had one. Their wide, flat-bottomed hulls made them suitable for dredging oysters.

The skipjacks were the signature boat of the bay's oyster fleet. Slightly smaller than the bugeyes, they likely first began appearing on the bay during the early 1890s, just as the oyster business was exploding. Skipjacks, because they have straight bottoms and flat sides, were easy to build.[413] Most watermen, certainly those at the turn of the twentieth century, had the knowhow needed to build them. What made them perform so well in a breeze was a deadrise, which gave them a distinctive V-shaped bottom.[414] This enabled them to sail closer to the wind and come about more with less effort. A centerboard that could be raised or lowered enabled them to work in shallow water.[415] For ballast, fieldstones, sometimes two tons of stone, were added. Having a draft of only two to three feet, the skipjack was ideal for working the bay's shallow waters.[416]

18

ICE IN THE BAY

2000s

BIG ICE YEARS IN THE EARLY 2000s

In the last forty-four years, there have been no repeats of 1977's massive ice cover in the Chesapeake. However, ice cover necessitating the use of U.S. Coast Guard cutters and tugs to open channels has occurred with some regularity. In the first twenty years of the current century, ice clogged the upper bay during the winters of 2002–03, 2003–04, 2008–09, 2009–10, 2013–14, 2014–15, 2017–18 and 2018–19. In the freezing cold winters of 2014–15 and 2017–18, an open pack ice extended south to the Chesapeake Bay Bridge and beyond to the mouth of the Potomac River. Both Smith Island and Tangier Island required tugs and cutters to open the ice and to deliver fuel oil and perishable goods. The iciest winters thus far this century are discussed in some detail here.[417]

THE WINTER OF 2003–04

In late January 2004, thick ice covered the upper bay. For example, the ice's thicknesses between Howell Point and Warton Point ranged from twelve to twenty inches. The coast guard positioned three of its icebreakers north of Baltimore to assist with icebreaking operations, keeping channels open to permit the safe passage of large and small boats alike, and replacing disabled buoys. Even so, it took the cruise ship *Haul Oceania* nearly two hours to travel approximately ten miles from Tolchester to Grove Point on its way to the

Left: A MODerate Resolution Imaging Satellite (MODIS) image showing ice in the Chesapeake Bay on February 11, 2010, following two record snowstorms. *Courtesy of NASA.*

Opposite: A MODIS image showing ice in the Chesapeake Bay on January 20, 2014. *Courtesy of NASA.*

Chesapeake and Delaware Canal.[418] As far south as the Chesapeake Bay Bridge, lanes through the ice were carved to assist ships that were picking up cargo and unloading goods in Baltimore Harbor.

The thickness and hardness of the ice was approaching the limit of what the coast guard's icebreakers could handle. Snow falling on top of existing ice made cutting more taxing, as the new snow essentially added to the ice's thickness. Ice extended from shore to shore in the bay's upper reaches. The nineteen-member crew of the *Frank Drew*, a nine-hundred-ton cutter commissioned in 2000, broke ice for ten consecutive days in late January and early February.[419] The cutter's twin one-thousand-horsepower propellers had little difficulty breaking through newly formed ice, but cutting brash ice (refrozen shards of previously broken ice) and ridge ice (where pressure forces the ice to ridge) was no easy chore. This ice actually scrapes away the ship's paint. In fact, traces of paint often coat ice that has been freshly cut.[420]

Not only do boats and barges utilize the paths cleared by the cutter, but also bald eagles and seabirds quickly learn to flock overhead in order to gain quick access to fish. In years when ice is severe, these paths are lifelines to eagles, which will migrate farther south if no other open water is available.[421]

THE WINTER OF 2014–15

The winter of 2014–15 was the iciest in the Chesapeake Bay in thirty-six years. Temperatures in February 2015 rivaled those experienced in February 1979. In both months, a well-developed upper-atmospheric ridge in the West (over the Pacific coast) and a trough that was set up over central Canada allowed arctic air to pour south, into the northern plains of the United States. From

A Vane Brothers tug in the upper Chesapeake Bay (photograph taken in the winter of 2010). *Courtesy of Vane Brothers.*

A Vane Brothers buoy in the Chesapeake Bay near the Patapsco River (photograph taken in February 2015). *Courtesy of Vane Brothers.*

there, it spread over the Midwest, the Great Lakes, New England and the Mid-Atlantic region. In 2015, as the polar vortex strengthened, it enhanced the meandering of the jet stream over eastern North America, permitting cold air to be routed well into the middle latitudes.[422]

Air temperatures in the bay area during the preceding fall were actually slightly above normal. Although January temperatures were below normal, the coldest air of the season did not arrive until February. It remained consistently cold throughout much of March.

Water temperatures in early winter through the midwinter, though they were slightly above normal until late January, were cold enough for freezing to occur once the polar air settled in early February. In most winters, with the water temperature still several degrees above freezing into late January, little or no ice will form. But because February 2015 was so cold, ice formed over the less salty water of the upper bay quite quickly. By mid-February, the ice had reached the mid-bay, and by late February, as water temperatures continued to fall, ice in the open bay extended toward the mouth of the Potomac River. Additionally, ice solidly covered the tributaries leading into the lower bay. At the Baltimore Harbor, the water temperature fell to 31.7° Fahrenheit on February 20.

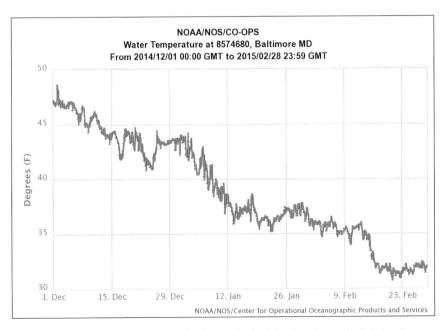

A chart showing water temperatures (Baltimore Harbor) for the winter of 2014–15. *Courtesy of NOAA/NOS/Center for Operational Oceanographic Products and Services.*

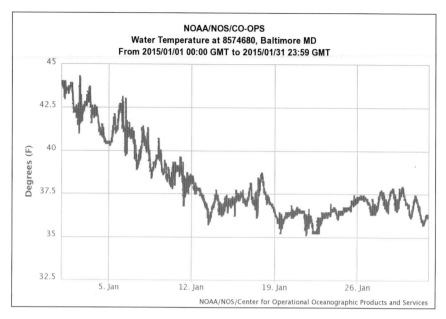

A chart showing water temperatures (Baltimore Harbor) for January 2015. *Courtesy of NOAA/NOS/Center for Operational Oceanographic Products and Services.*

The four vessels owned by Maryland's Department of Natural Resources were all employed for icebreaking duties.[423] Moreover, in Delaware Bay, the ice pack was so thick that the Cape May–Lewes Ferry had to suspend service for several days in late February.[424]

According to long-term records, February 2015 was the second-coldest month observed in the eastern North American region, including the Chesapeake Bay area, since 1900.[425]

THE WINTER OF 2017–18

The late fall and winter of 2017–18 was quite chilly in the Chesapeake Bay region. Although the temperatures each month from November to February were slightly below normal, this winter was remarkable for its extreme cold in late December and early January. The first week of January was the coldest first week of the new year ever recorded at most observing stations. At several locations, the temperature did not exceed 20° Fahrenheit for three consecutive days, and at Baltimore, the temperature remained below

A MODIS image showing ice in the Chesapeake Bay on February 18, 2015. *Courtesy of NASA.*

freezing for eight consecutive days, the longest such stretch since 1990. As ice began to build, Maryland's four ice cutters responded.[426]

By early January, ice thicknesses of five inches were observed alongshore at Crisfield. In Tangier Sound, freezing was becoming a problem for navigation, but most boats were able to transit the bay's main channel on their own, as it is deeper and saltier than waters near the shore. However, barges carrying fuel oil were required to trail an icebreaker, clearing a path to the fuel docks in Crisfield.[427] In Annapolis, Spa Creek iced over completely in just two days, requiring the icebreaker *Widener* to carve a track into Annapolis Harbor. On January 16, the water temperature in

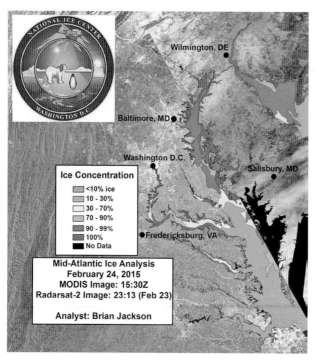

This page, top: Ice concentrations in the Chesapeake Bay and Delaware Bay on February 24, 2015. *Courtesy of the National Snow and Ice Data Center.*

This page, bottom: A MODIS image showing ice in the Chesapeake Bay on March 6, 2015. *Courtesy of NASA.*

Opposite: A Vane Brothers tug opening a path on the frozen Wicomico River. This photograph was taken in January 2018. *Courtesy of Vane Brothers.*

Top: A Vane Brothers tugboat, the *Falcon*, pushing a barge through the ice on the Wicomico River. This photograph was taken in January 2018. *Courtesy of Vane Brothers.*

Bottom: A Vane Brothers tug breaking ice in the Wicomico River. This photograph was taken in January 2018. *Courtesy of Vane Brothers.*

Baltimore Harbor was 31.8° Fahrenheit, the lowest recorded for the winter. Recall that in 2015, the harbor water was not at its coldest until February 20.[428]

In the bay waters of Virginia, oyster season, which typically closes at the end of April, was extended for a week because, in some places, boats had been iced in for nearly two weeks. According to the Virginia Marine Resources Commission, there were eighteen days that winter when watermen were impacted by the ice, and for nine of those days, no oysters were "officially" harvested.[429]

Right: A MODIS image showing ice in the Chesapeake Bay on January 7, 2018. *Courtesy of NASA.*

Below: Shore ice in the lower Rappahannock River of Virginia. *Courtesy of Patricia Cooley, photographer.*

The ice was so frozen around Tangier Island that it was inaccessible by boat as early as January 3.[430] Food and supplies had to be brought in by air on two UH-60 Black Hawk helicopters. It seems that one of the most requested food items was cat food. With more than five hundred cats on the island, felines outnumber their human caretakers.

A stranded visitor to the island mentioned that he observed more than one hundred residents sledding, skating and socializing near a bonfire at Jobs Cove, a wintertime tradition that was last celebrated during the winter of 1976–77. One longtime island resident said that even though the ice surrounding the island was thick, the skin of people living on the island was thicker. Neighbors were helping each other, and most residents learned to prepare for this sort of event by making sure they had a well-stocked freezer.[431]

By late January, temperatures eased and were above normal for the remainder of the month, allowing the ice to gradually melt. In February, temperatures fell again, but the ice that reformed was not a concern for watermen or shippers.

KEEPING THE BAY AND ITS WATERWAYS OPEN

Just a degree or two of temperature difference can determine if ice will form and if the ice will become thick enough to halt vessel traffic. Ice can weaken quickly during a thaw, and it can harden just as quickly with a falling thermometer. The MDNR buoy tenders and tugs and U.S. Coast Guard cutters are charged with keeping the bay open when ice becomes an issue. The MDNR boats include the *Widener*, the *Sandusky*, the *Big Lou* (a tugboat) and the *J. Millard Tawes*, the largest of the four at one hundred feet in length and with an icebreaking draft (width) of eighteen feet.[432]

Icebreaking is primarily conducted to support the commercial activities needed to provide services to the communities on the bay and its tributaries. Ice conditions are given three levels of readiness, with ice condition 3 having the least severe ice and ice condition 1 having the worst.

Condition 3: Readiness. Temperatures favorable for ice development in navigable waters.[433]

Condition 2: Alert. Appreciable ice forms and noteworthy thickness and coverage occurs in the upper bay, the Chesapeake and Delaware Canal, the upper Potomac River and on the Maryland Eastern Shore; reconnaissance begins; waterway restrictions may be imposed (includes, but not limited to, steel-hulled only, minimum total horsepower, tug accompaniment, daylight/ one-way transits only).[434]

Condition 1: Emergency. Severe ice exists; further restrictions imposed; convoys are required. The coast guard sets winter port condition 1 (ice condition 1). The last time this condition was met was in January 2018.

BREAKING ICE

In years when the bay is iced over, the MDNR boats are crucial in keeping a supply line open to Smith and Tangier Islands, where everything that goes in or out relies on open water. Since schools for the island's students are located in Crisfield (Somerset County) on Maryland's southern Eastern Shore over nine miles from Smith Island, making sure these students attend class during periods when ice conditions are severe also falls on the reinforced hulls of the icebreakers. In exceptional and epic ice seasons—such as in 1918, 1936, 1977, 1979 and 2015—and also in other winters when the ice is especially thick, U.S. Coast Guard icebreakers are brought in to help keep the bay navigable. Furthermore, breakers owned by private companies, including Vane Brothers and Curtis Bay Towing, are also employed to help break the ice.[435]

When ice conditions are severe, convoys led by cutters and tugs are mandated by the MDNR to assist barges and their tows heading from Baltimore to and through the Chesapeake and Delaware Canal, for example. Tugs with less than one thousand horsepower are underpowered for severe ice and are barred from these convoys.[436]

Icebreaking is about power, not finesse. Coast guard cutters have propeller blades that depend on the size of the vessel, which may be 140 feet long and 37 feet wide. In theory, the larger and wider the ship the larger the channel it will cut. The rounded hull of these iceboats is designed to ride up on the ice. Whether these ships are breaking ice on the Chesapeake or in the arctic, the strategy is simply to smash the ice with the force of the ships' massive weights.[437]

A well-designed hull will move the ice aside once it has been busted. If the ice is especially hard and thick, a seasoned captain can reverse the engine and then ram forward. By shifting the ballast from one compartment to another, the ship can actually move slightly from side to side.[438] In some ways, the effort involved is similar to freeing your car from snow and ice.

A Vane Brothers tugboat, the *Carlyn*, moving through ice near Baltimore. This photograph was taken in February 2019. *Courtesy of Vane Brothers.*

An approach introduced in the second half of the twentieth century involves using a compressor to blow bubbles of air below the waterline. These bubbles then act as a lubricant, helping the ship slide through the ice—not exactly like a hot knife through butter, but that is the hope. Of course, a knife in butter is silent; an icebreaker crushing ice is anything but. Like a train on uneven rails, it wobbles and shudders, and the noise can be unnerving.[439]

The ice groans, cracks and creaks. The sound of breaking ice aboard ship is loud and, on occasion, alarmingly so. Grinding and snapping sounds may even awaken seasoned sailors from their slumber. A full day on the bay breaking ice can take a toll on the ship's crew.

ANOTHER LOOK AT THE BIG ICE YEARS ON THE BAY

I ce forms in the colder, fresher waters of the upper Chesapeake Bay nearly every winter. As a rule of thumb, ice in the upper bay is a concern for navigation and commercial fishing every six or seven years. Chesapeake Bay ice is, of course, more interesting and more widely reported following a period of consecutive years when the bay's waters have been generally ice-free—for example, after the icy winter of 1919–20, the bay was not significantly icy again until the winter of 1935–36.

Because the average air temperature in the bay area, even in the coldest months, January and February, is above 32° Fahrenheit, prolonged cold is required to ice over the mid- and lower bay areas. However, even in relatively warm winters, ice will form if polar air cools the surface water to the freezing level, but in these instances, the ice cover is more of a veneer instead of a solid covering. On the other hand, in winters when air temperatures are below normal but winds are persistent, ice formation may be delayed. But if air temperatures during autumn are cool and the bay's waters are below their normal temperature entering winter, the average air temperature in January is a bellwether in determining how severe the icing will become.[440]

It is interesting to observe that during the years when the ice coverage was well above normal, even during the epic icing events of the past four hundred years, the air temperatures following the melt (in early spring) on both the western shore and Eastern Shore of the Chesapeake Bay did not seem to be affected by the icy waters that winter. In Baltimore, as an example, there is virtually no connection between the maximum winter ice extent in January and February and the air temperature in March. Since 1900, for the years with the iciest winters, only in 1904 and in 2015 was the air temperature in March considered colder than normal. In essence, it seems that after an exceptionally cold winter, the atmosphere is spent; the jet stream migrates to the north, shutting off cold air to the Mid-Atlantic region.

Therefore, it should not be surprising that there is little persistence between the severity of the winter and spring and summer temperatures; a cold winter does not portend a cool, pleasant summer. "If there is spring in winter and winter in spring, the year won't be good for anything." In the spring of 2020, a nippy April and May followed on the heels of one of the mildest winters in the Chesapeake region. In the northern and even the central portions of the Chesapeake's watershed, snow flurries were observed on May 9—one of the latest notations of snow in one of the least-snowy winters on record.

In 1918, nearly the entire bay was frozen in January, but the temperature soared to record levels that summer, reaching 105° Fahrenheit in August in Baltimore. Moreover, though the winter of 1936 was bone-chilling, record-breaking heat was experienced in Maryland and Virginia during July and August.[441] During the winter of 1685–86 in New England, it was said that the frozen sacramental bread rattled on the plate as it was being passed.[442] However, this hard winter was followed by a great drought—fires in the swamps burned underground to a depth of six feet. Similarly, the abysmal winter of 1696–97 was followed by a warm and very dry summer, and again, in October, the forests burned.[443]

There is also not an obvious association between the severity of the cold or the extent of the ice in a given winter and conditions during either the winter before or the winter after. In 1635, for instance, it was mentioned in letters that "this last winter was the coldest that has been knowne in many yeeres: but the yeere before, there was scarce any signe of winter, onely that the leaves fell from the trees, in all other things it appeared to be summer."[444]

THE BIGGEST ICE YEARS

January is generally the month that has the greatest ice extent. But in several big ice years, the maximum ice extent occurred in February, like in February 1895, 1899, 1978, 1979 and 2015.[445]

Air temperatures have noticeably warmed in recent decades. Still, in almost every winter, there is a period of a few days to a few weeks when the average air temperature in the bay region remains below freezing. Ice will form in the bay then but perhaps only in the upper bay and perhaps only for a few days or so. On occasion, however, cold arctic air pours across the upper Midwest and into the eastern United States nearly uninterrupted for weeks at a time. These are the winters in which the ice cover in the Chesapeake Bay becomes "severe" or, if the cold is prolonged, "exceptional." Yet, when autumn temperatures are much lower than normal and the arctic air is in place in early winter, the bay water will become prechilled. During these rare winters, for this chronicle, the icing that occurs is deemed to be "epic." (See tables 3 and 4.) Since 1800, there have been five such epic winters: 1835–36, 1856–57, 1892–93, 1917–18 and 1976–77. Between 1600 and 1800—though it is not known with a high degree of certainty—it is believed that the winters of 1641–42, 1645–46, 1697–98, 1740–41, 1749–50, 1779–80 and 1783–84 all experienced epic cold conditions. During these winters, for at least a two-week period, 75 percent or more of the Chesapeake Bay was covered in ice. In all likelihood, the surface weather conditions, as well as the upper air circulation, from October to February, for all of these winters featured similar patterns and positions.

Only during the satellite era (since the 1960s) have we been able to reliably measure and monitor the growth and expanse of ice in the bay. But in the 1970s and 1980s, satellites with the resolution to adequately observe the Chesapeake Bay (the Landsat series of satellites) did not make observations on a daily basis. Additionally, when images are acquired, with sensors observing only in the visible portion of the electromagnetic spectrum, clouds often restrict viewing opportunities—a clear satellite view of the bay may only be available every ten days or longer. Thus, in many instances, the satellite-derived areal extent of the ice can only be estimated. For example, in early February 1977, approximately 85 percent of the Chesapeake Bay was iced over, as determined by relatively cloud-free Landsat satellite images of the bay that were acquired on February 1 and 2 of that year. Therefore, for comparison purposes, 1977, as well as the other epic years that came before it, are all judged to have had a maximum ice coverage for a two-week period of at least 75 percent.

The timeline of the largest ice years (epic ice years) in the Chesapeake Bay from 1600 to 2020 is shown on page 166. As was mentioned in chapter 4, the Little Ice Age conditions affected eastern North America during the seventeenth and eighteenth centuries. Not every winter was cold, but a number of winters were significantly colder than they were in the two previous centuries and the two centuries that followed. However, from looking

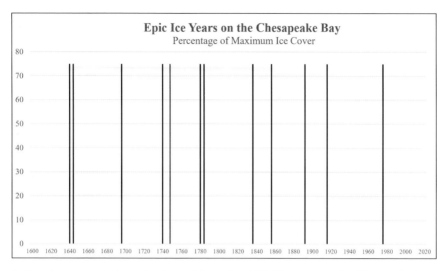

Epic Ice Years on the Chesapeake Bay
Percentage of Maximum Ice Cover

A plot of ice cover during epic winters (winters in which 75 percent of the Chesapeake Bay is ice-covered) in the Chesapeake Bay from 1600–2020. *Author's collection.*

at this plot, even though there were more epic ice years before 1800 than there have been in the 220 years that followed, the spread is not particularly conspicuous. The greatest separation between any two epic winters is fifty-two years—between the winters of 1645–46 and 1697–98 and the winters of 1783–84 and 1835–36. On three other occasions, more than forty years passed between epic winters—1697–98 to 1740–41; 1917–18 to 1976–77; and 1976–77 to the present.

If each winter was plotted when the bay ice was severe (ice extended to the middle of the mid-bay), a more perceptible trend would result. Such a plot cannot be accurately depicted, since in the early part of the record, there were likely winters in which the ice was significant for several weeks that were just not mentioned in letters and diaries.[446]

THE YEARS AHEAD

With continued warming, will an extensive ice cover on the Chesapeake Bay become a thing of the past? Judging from the historical record, it would seem that even if the average annual temperature in the Mid-Atlantic region increases by 3.5° Fahrenheit (approximately 2° Celsius) by the end of the twenty-first century, on occasion ice would still be notable in the bay.

At present, as average temperatures during the coldest months of the year in the eastern United States are more than 1° Fahrenheit warmer than the average temperatures in the 1970s, there are still years in which the ice cover that forms on bodies of water—the Great Lakes for example—greatly exceeds the normal winter ice extent.[447] Considerably more ice than normal was observed in 2014, 2015 and 2018. However, since 1973, a trend toward diminishing ice cover has been noted in the Great Lakes.[448] Also, the maximum areal snow cover extent for North America in the winter season has not changed substantially in the last forty years—winters are generally warmer, but the average position of the 32° Fahrenheit isotherm in mid-January has not shifted significantly to the north.[449]

As ice covers at least a portion of the upper bay during most winters, its frequency of occurrence there would be expected to decline as winter temperatures rise. Even so, regardless of whether the global average temperature increases—2°, 3° or as much as 4° Fahrenheit—by the end of the century, bitter cold air will now and then invade the middle latitudes. When it does, and if temperatures average below freezing (32° Fahrenheit) for an extended period, conversations will lead with, "Can you believe the bay is frozen up?"

From looking at the timeline of average wintertime minimum temperatures for the state of Maryland from 1895 to 2014, there is appreciable variance in the long-term trend. Note that even as air temperatures have warmed, the average minimum temperature in several recent winters has been well below the long-term trend line. Though none have been nearly as cold as the temperatures observed in the late 1970s, several winters since the mid-1990s,

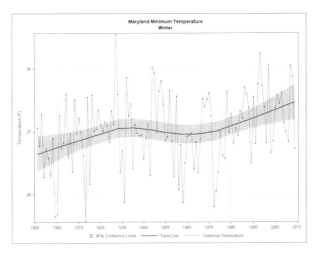

A plot of average minimum temperatures for selected meteorological stations in Maryland from 1896–2014. *Courtesy of the Maryland State Climatologist Office.*

including 2014–15 (not included on timeline), have been as icy as the ones represented in the earlier part of the graph (1895–1915).[450]

Therefore, although there is a likelihood that there will be fewer episodes of icing later this century than there were at the end of the eighteenth, nineteenth and twentieth centuries, it is expected that there will still be an occasional exceptional winter—when ice covers the entirety of the upper bay and completely covers the mid-bay as it did in 1903–04, 1904–05, 1916–17, 1935–36, 1960–61, 1978–79 and 2014–15.

During each of the last four centuries, there have been at least two winters in which ice has had a stranglehold on the entire Chesapeake Bay. As of this writing, it has been forty-four years since the bay's last epic ice year. Will we see another winter like that of 1976–77 before the twenty-second century begins? For the reasons stated above, it would be reasonable to prognosticate that at least one epic icy winter will be observed on the Chesapeake Bay by the year 2100.

ICE ON THE CHESAPEAKE

From Turkey Point to the outbound Capes and back again to town
The bay ice swept in crystal shapes, with the white snow for a crown.
It was, Bring the ice boats, let 'em heave! and with mighty strength they drove—
From Sassafras and the Pocomoke, from the Elk to Walnut Cove!
No shipping there on the long white trail, no stream and not a sail;
Lost seagulls struggling against the waste and the sound of a sirens wail.
From Seven Foot Knoll to Magothy Light, from Drum Point to the sea,
A welter of white in the star-bright light the Chesapeake showed to me.
Wind and snow and a cutting chill and the tide cracks of that wonder
Come rolling home beneath the dome like the crash of April thunder.
Lost ducks sitting along the shore and the channel lights so low—
And no ship in for Baltimore since three long weeks ago![451]

APPENDICES

APPENDIX A
MORE ON THE GEOGRAPHY OF THE CHESAPEAKE BAY

We know that the orientation of the Chesapeake Bay (cool, fresh water flowing into the bay from the north) is conducive to ice formation when the weather turns cold. But what would ice conditions be like if the bay's current configuration was flipped (for example, if the bay's entrance to the Atlantic was near its current northernmost latitude and the river providing the bulk of its fresh water flowed from south to north, entering the bay near its current southernmost latitude)? For this hypothetical "Chesapeake Bay," ice would form only in its northern tributaries in most years; the lower freezing point of salt water, tidal swash and faster-flowing currents all act to retard the freezing of the open water in the upper bay region.

But the southern source of the hypothetical river providing most of the freshwater inflow to the bay would be several degrees warmer than river water entering the bay from the present Susquehanna. Nevertheless, water temperatures in the lower bay would be cooler than those experienced today, and icing would occur more frequently. In this flipped version of the Chesapeake Bay, during an exceptionally cold winter, the bay could still freeze over. In such winters, once the entrance to the Atlantic was frozen, the entire bay could then freeze—much like an inland lake.

APPENDIX B
MORE ABOUT THE FREEZING OF THE BAY'S WATERS

Ice that has softened, under the right conditions, may compress, becoming even thicker and harder than it was originally. Once broken, the ice can refreeze so that it is harder than it was before, even if temperatures are just below the freezing mark. Constant refreezing makes for very strong ice—ice that is hard to cut through. For instance, ice that was passable during the daylight hours when temperatures approach 40° Fahrenheit can become extremely hard after sunset, when the thermometer dips into the twenties (degrees Fahrenheit) and the bay water temperature drops to the freezing level. Virgin ice—ice that has not melted and refrozen—will actually be relatively easy to break and maneuver through compared to the refrozen ice.

APPENDIX C
ICEBREAKING AND NAVIGATING THE BAY'S ICE

In regard to ice and vessel size, deeper drafts mean there will be less surface ice drawn into the ships' strainers.[452] In ice-clogged waters, even a smaller boat should stay within deeper channels, because if it becomes locked up in ice, it will be much more difficult for a cutter or tug to free it.

Even when a pathway is made through pack ice, because this ice is in motion, the opening can quickly shift. Therefore, boats and barges must be careful to follow the shifting open pathway; otherwise, they may find themselves seriously stuck in pack ice. However, if this open path drifts over an area where the channel is shallow, the pilot must be aware of this; navigation charts must still be paid attention to.

The bow of an icebreaking vessel acts as a wedge as it's driven into the ice. If the ice does not have a place to move, it will exert pressure on the vessel's hull. If the force exerted by the ice is equal to or stronger than the propeller force of the vessel, the vessel will grind to a halt. Though the horsepower of a vessel is important in breaking ice, the hull design is critical as well. Ships with narrow bows and relatively short midsections will enter the ice and clear it more readily than wider-beamed bows with longer mid-sections. Pointed bows cut the ice and allow it to move away along the vessel's hull.

Tugs can have their ballasts positioned so that their bows are high, permitting them to ride on the ice and break through it. In this way, the screw resides deeper in the water and is not as subject to ice damage. Also, tugs perform better if their sterns are ellipse-shaped, as this makes it easier to turn in heavy ice concentrations than more square-shaped sterns. Plus, vessels that have heavier loads or deeper drafts will move through ice better than shallow-drafted vessels, as more resistance (more ice) is required to stop these heavier ships.

In the Chesapeake Bay, tugboats typically operate between four hundred and seven thousand horsepower, whereas large ships navigating the bay may approach sixty thousand horsepower. So, tugs are at a huge disadvantage compared to these larger ships moving through thick ice fields. However, tugs and their tows have drafts that rarely exceed fifteen feet, and in the bay's shallow waters, this is an advantage that helps them navigate ice that forms outside the deeper channels and closer to shore.

During icebreaking activities, the ice is classified by its concentration, type and topography. Regarding its concentration, ice is listed to the nearest 10 percent coverage or as "no ice." Thickness is reported in inches. Several different types of ice are encountered. These include new ice (newly formed since the previous observation), frazil ice, fast ice, pack ice, pancake ice and other (any other ice accumulations).

As ice conditions become more dangerous, the ice may attain topography, including rafting (pieces pushing together and overriding one another), ridging (connected pack ice sections and refrozen leads), hummocking (piles of ice pressed into a jagged mass).

Below is an example of the ice reports issued by the U.S. Coast Guard when the bay is icy—as it was in the winter of 1978 (only selected days and selected bay and river locations are listed here).

January 11, 1978

General condition for the upper bay—scattered sheet and compact ice.

Specific conditions (from north to south): Chesapeake and Delaware Canal—⅞ coverage, 4 inches, compact ice; Magothy River—⅜ coverage, ½ inch, pancake ice; Potomac River (entrance)—⅛ coverage, ½ inch, pancake ice.

February 16, 1978

General conditions for the upper bay— 5/6 coverage, 3–8 inches, compact ice. Shipping channels are easy to moderate to transit, no horsepower limitations.

Specific conditions (from north to south): Elk River—8/8 coverage, 10 inch, compact ice; Chesapeake and Delaware Canal—8/8 coverage, 6–8 inches, rafting; Magothy River—8/8 coverage, 5 inches, fast ice; Chester River (entrance)—8/8 coverage, 3 inches, compact ice; Severn River—8/8 coverage, 5 inches, fast ice; Potomac River (entrance to Piney Point)—6/8 coverage, 5–12 inches, floes; (Alexandria, Virginia, to Washington, D.C.)—6/8 coverage, 1 inch, brash ice.

Planned convoys and requested assistance—coast guard cutter *Capstan* attempting to break out watermen in St. Mary's River (Potomac tributary). Also assisting tug *Popa* tow two barges and assist two private yachts.

March 6, 1978

General conditions for the upper bay—limited ice.

Specific conditions (from north to south): Elk River—8/8 coverage, 4 inches, compact ice; Chesapeake and Delaware Canal—⅛ coverage, 1 inch, compact ice; Magothy River—8/8 coverage, 5 inches, fast ice; Chester River (entrance)—⅜ coverage, 1–2 inches, open pack ice; Severn River—limited ice; Potomac River (entrance and channel to Washington, D.C.)—limited ice.

APPENDIX D:
COMPARISON OF THE THREE CONSECUTIVE COLD WINTERS; 1976–77, 1977–78 AND 1978–79

Freshwater ice growth is closely related to the accumulation of freezing degree days (FDD), defined as the negative departure of the mean daily air temperature (32° Fahrenheit). This metric provides an additional way (in addition to air temperature and water temperature) to compare how cold

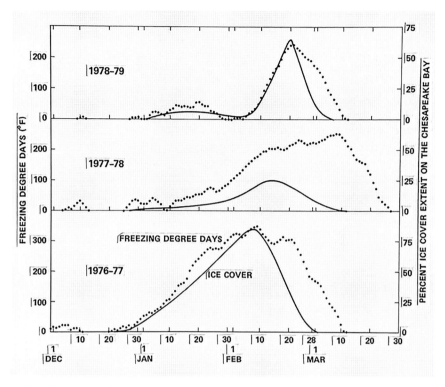

A plot of cumulative freezing degree days (Baltimore, Maryland) and ice extent for the winters of 1976–77, 1977–78 and 1978–79. *Author's collection.*

one season or year is to another. Since the average air temperature during the coldest months is above 32° Fahrenheit in most locations around the Chesapeake Bay, FDD accumulations are often negligible during the winter season. However, as seen from the plot on this page, FDD accumulations were considerable during the winters of 1976–77, 1977–78 and 1978–79.

Based on satellite observations, the maximum ice cover in the bay occurred around the same time as the peak FDD accumulation during the winters of 1976–77 and 1978–79. But in 1977–78, the maximum ice cover extent occurred in mid-February, which was about three weeks earlier than the peak FDD accumulation (March 8). Evidently, a brief thaw in mid-February broke up the ice cover. Note that during the winter of 1977–78, the peak FDD accumulation was reached around the same time that the FDD accumulation approached zero during the winters of 1976–77 and 1978–79.

During the winter of 1977–78, there were ninety-two days in which the accumulated FDD remained above zero, compared to just eighty-two days for the winter of 1976–77 and seventy-five days for 1978–79. Not surprisingly, ice cover remained on the bay longer during the winter of 1977–78 than the other two winters. Note, though, that the maximum ice cover was much more extensive in 1976–77 than in 1977–78.

A total accumulation of 350 FDD was recorded during the winter of 1976–77, compared to 255 for 1977–78 and 245 for 1978–79, demonstrating the importance of total accumulation of FDD in determining the severity of ice conditions. Of note is that during the winter of 1978–79, the ice cover was somewhat more extensive than during 1977–78, even though the accumulation of total FDD was slightly less. This is attributed to the record-breaking cold of February 1979 that resulted in the upper bay freezing over in approximately one week's time. Looking again at this plot, in February 1979, the accumulation of FDD was near 0 on February 4 and peaked at 245 only seventeen days later, on February 21. But during the winter of 1977–78, fifty-eight days were required for FDD to accumulate from near 0 on January 9 to the peak of 255 on March 8.

It should be noted that the steepest portions of the slopes on the FDD curves are the times of maximum cooling and ice formation. For the winter of 1976–77, the most rapid cooling occurred between December 28 and January 24, and for the winter of 1978–79, it occurred between February 4 and February 23. The more gradual slope of the curve during the winter of 1977–78 indicates the slower rate of ice growth that occurred during this winter, when the maximum cooling occurred between January 26 and February 13. For these three winters, their coldest portions occurred later in each subsequent year. Correspondingly, the time of maximum ice cover extent occurred about a week later from one year to the next.

Also illustrated in the figure on page 175, the ice cover curve, during melt, falls off more rapidly than the FDD curve, since the FDD curve is cumulative and, hence, does not represent the freezing line or the average daily temperature.

NOTES

Chapter 1

1. Fisher, "My Chesapeake," 428–67.
2. Kenney, "Chesapeake Country."
3. Ibid.
4. Miers, *Drowned River*, 6.
5. USGS, "Largest Rivers."
6. Barry, *Susquehanna River Valley*, 126.
7. Bay Trippers.
8. Chesapeake Bay Program, "Geography."
9. Ibid.
10. Fisher, "My Chesapeake," 428–67.
11. Hoffman, "Who's Killing?"; McGrath and Hager, "American Treasure."

Chapter 2

12. Job 37:10.
13. Davis, *Science Nuggets*, 69–70.
14. Matthews, "Ice on the World," 79–119.
15. When salt water freezes, minute pockets of brine are trapped between crystals of ice. If the ice thickens over the winter, gravity moves the brine downward so that most of the ice cover, when it melts, will be fresh water.
16. Canby, "Weather Went Wild," 798–829.

Chapter 3

17. Hall, *Narratives, 1633–16*, 348; Written in a pamphlet in 1666 by George Alsop. This was likely encouraged by Lord Baltimore as an inducement for servants to come to Maryland. Alsop served as an indentured servant on a plantation in Baltimore County, Maryland, for four years.
18. Footner, *Rivers of the Eastern Shore*, 11–13.
19. Earle, "The Great Bay," 251.
20. J.G.S., "Early Spanish Explorations."
21. Ibid.
22. Footner, *Rivers of the Eastern Shore*, 13–14.
23. National Park Service, "John Smith's Journals."
24. Chesapeake Bay Program, "Captain John Smith."
25. Hall, *Narratives, 1633–16*, 67.
26. Ibid., 77, 78; Derived partly by the commissioners of the colony of Maryland under the instructions from the proprietary, which every ship was required to send when departing from the province.
27. Karen Ordahl Kupperman, "Seventeenth Century New England: Climate and Mastery of the Wilderness in Seventeenth-Century New England," *Colonial Society of Massachusetts* 63 (2017): n.p.
28. A verse from Samuel Sewall's "Verses Upon New Century" (Massachusetts Historical Society, "Massachusetts Historical Society Papers: Samuel Sewall Diary, 1685–1703," www.masshist.org).

Chapter 4

29. Kupperman, "Seventeenth Century New England."
30. Ibid.
31. Massachusetts Society Historical Papers, the Winthrop Papers Digital Edition, Papers of the Winthrop, vol. 4., www.masshist.org.
32. Ibid.
33. Moody, "Thomas Gorges," 75:10–26.
34. Massachusetts Society Historical Papers, the Winthrop Papers Digital Edition, Papers of the Winthrop, vol. 4., www.masshist.org.
35. Moody, "Thomas Gorges," 75:10–26.
36. Kupperman, "Seventeenth Century New England."
37. Ibid.
38. Ibid.
39. Sommerville, "Early Career of Governor," 101–14.
40. Clayton, "A Letter," 17:781–95, 17:941–48, 18:121–35.
41. Perhaps this was during the winter of 1686–87 or the winter of 1656–57.
42. Ludlum, *American Winters, 1604–1820*, 162–63.
43. Massachusetts Historical Society, "Samuel Sewall Diary."

44. Kalm, a Swedish naturalist, visited the American colonies near the middle of the eighteenth century; Kalm, *En Rasa til Norra America*.
45. Kupperman, "Seventeenth Century New England."

Chapter 5

46. These winters include 1707–8, 1711–12, 1725–26, 1726–27, 1727–28, 1743–35, 1751–52, 1756–57, 1760–61, 1761–62, 1763–64, 1771–72, 1781–82, 1784–85, 1786–87 and 1791–92.
47. Ludlum, *American Winters, 1604–1820*, 162–63.
48. Middleton, *Tobacco Coast*, 482.
49. Ibid., 145.
50. Kalm, *En Rasa til Norra America*, n.p.
51. Ibid.
52. Ibid.
53. *Annapolis Gazette*, October 25, 1749.
54. Kalm, *En Rasa til Norra America*, n.p.
55. Ibid.
56. Ludlum, *American Winters I, 1604–1820*, 162–63.
57. *Maryland Gazette* (Annapolis), January 1761.
58. "Deposition," *Maryland Historical Magazine*.
59. *Maryland Gazette* (Annapolis), January 28, 1780; *Virginia Gazette* (Williamsburg), January 22 and 29, 1780, and February 5, 1780; Healy, *Great Storms*, 45.
60. Skaggs and Macmaster, "Post-Revolutionary Letters."
61. Ibid.
62. Healy, *Great Storms*, 45; Scharf, *Chronicles of Baltimore*, 235.
63. Shomette, *Shipwrecks*, 75–85; *Maryland Gazette* (Annapolis), February 5 and 12, 1784.
64. *Maryland Gazette* (Annapolis), March 11, 1784.
65. *Virginia Gazette* (Williamsburg), January 31, 1784; *Virginia Journal and Alexandria Advertiser*, March 18, 1784.
66. Boyd, "James Madison to Thomas Jefferson," 6, 537.
67. Alexandria is across the Potomac River from Washington, D.C.; Georgetown is now a part of Washington, D.C.; Skaggs and Macmaster, "Post-Revolutionary Letters."
68. Dorsey, "Conduct of Business in Baltimore."
69. Ibid.
70. Ibid.
71. Wood, *Tambora*, 293.
72. Ibid.; Franklin, "Meteorological Imaginations," 2, 357–61.
73. Wood, *Tambora*, 293; Franklin, "Meteorological Imaginations," 2, 357–61.
74. Howard, *Climate of London*, n.p.
75. Wood, *Tambora*, 293.
76. Lambert, "Travels of an English Immigrant."
77. Ibid.

78. Levin, "Barney Outwitted."
79. Ibid.
80. Kupperman, "Seventeenth Century New England."
81. Dr. Hugh Williamson's notes written in 1771.
82. Jefferson, *Notes*, n.p.
83. Ibid., 6, 512.
84. Webster, *A Collection of Papers*, 119.
85. Supplementary remarks were written and read before the same academy in 1806; Webster, *A Collection of Papers*, 148, 162.

Chapter 6

86. Unicorn Book Shop, "History of Maryland Weather."
87. Warden, "Journal of a Voyage."
88. "Diary of Egbert Gilmor," *Maryland Historical Magazine*; Emerson, "Book Review," 453.
89. "Diary of Egbert Gilmor," *Maryland Historical Magazine.*
90. "Brief History," *Chesapeake Bay Magazine.*
91. The U.S. Army Corps of Army Engineers designed and implemented this project.
92. American Society of Civil Engineers, "Chesapeake and Delaware Canal," 2020, www.asce.org.
93. John Maloney, "Chesapeake Odyssey," *National Geographic Magazine*, September 1939.
94. Ibid.
95. Brewington, "Chesapeake Bay Pilots."
96. Ludlum, *American Winters II, 1821–1870*, 16–20.
97. Niles, *Niles Weekly Register.*
98. Ibid., January 14, 1837.
99. Ibid., January 24, 1837.
100. Society of the Descendants of the Signers of the Declaration of Independence, "Charles Carroll of Carrollton," 2011, www.dsdi1776.com.
101. Hoffman, "Carroll Family," 331–50.
102. Ibid.
103. Colonel Carroll received the title "colonel" because he formed a military unit known as Carroll's Dragoons, which was organized to serve the State of Maryland as the national guard does today.
104. Byran Giemza, "Black, White and Irish in the South," *Southern Cultures* 18, no. 1 (Spring 2010): 34–57.
105. Pierre, "Treasured Islands."
106. S. Hartwell, "The Cat Fur Trade—Historical and Modern," 2015, www.messybeast.com.
107. Pierre, "Treasured Islands"; *Baltimore Sun*, January 5, 1847, 2.

108. *Baltimore Sun*, January 4, 1847.
109. See chapters 7 and 9.
110. *Baltimore Sun*, January 14, 1847.
111. Pierre, "Treasured Islands."
112. See chapter 18.
113. Ibid.
114. Cronin, *Disappearing Islands*, 200.
115. Pierre, "Treasured Islands."

Chapter 7

116. Ludlum, "Susquehanna Ice Bridge."
117. Healy, *Great Storms*, 158; *Mechanics' Magazine and Journal of Science, Arts and Manufacturers*, 455–56.
118. Diggins, "Bridging Port Deposit."
119. Ibid.
120. Ibid.
121. Ibid.
122. Ibid.
123. Miller, *Cecil County*, 173.
124. Wilson, W. B., 1889: History of the Pennsylvania Railroad, Philadelphia, PA.
125. *Mechanics' Magazine and Journal of Science, Arts and Manufacturers*, 455–56.
126. Miller, *Cecil County*, 173.
127. *Mechanics' Magazine and Journal of Science, Arts and Manufacturers*, 455–56.
128. Ibid.
129. Diggins, "Bridging Port Deposit."
130. Ibid.
131. Ibid.
132. Healy, *Great Storms*, 158.

Chapter 8

133. Ludlum, *American Winters II, 1821–1870*, 53–65.
134. Ruffin, "Diary of Edmund Ruffin."
135. *Times-Dispatch* (Richmond), January 24, 1958.
136. Ruffin, "Diary of Edmund Ruffin," 247.
137. Ibid.
138. Ibid.
139. Ibid.
140. Ibid.
141. Ludlum, *American Winters II, 1821–1870*, 53–65.

142. Ibid.; *Times-Dispatch* (Richmond), January 24, 1958.
143. Ruffin, "Diary of Edmund Ruffin," 247; Ludlum, *American Winters II, 1821–1870*, 230–33.
144. *Maryland Weather Service, 1899*, n.p.
145. Ibid.
146. *Baltimore Sun*, January 12, 1893.
147. See chapters 12 and 17.
148. "Icebound at Annapolis," *Baltimore Sun*, January 14, 1893.
149. "Old Winters Outdone," *Baltimore Sun*, January 16, 1893.
150. "Ice on the Chesapeake," *Baltimore Sun*, January 12, 1893.
151. "Old Winters," *Baltimore Sun*.
152. Ibid.
153. Reno, "Cold Enough."
154. *Maryland Weather Service, 1899*, n.p.
155. Foster and Leffler, "Extreme Weather."
156. Ibid.
157. *Maryland Weather Service, 1899*, n.p.
158. Foster and Leffler, "Extreme Weather."
159. Healy, *Great Storms*, 78–71.
160. Dodds, *Islands in a River*, 230; See chapters 12 and 17.
161. Ibid.
162. Ludlum, *American Weather Book*, 75; Scharf, *Chronicles of Baltimore*, 235.

Chapter 9

163. Hanicak, "Ice Gorges Terrorized."
164. The town of Lapidum no longer exists.
165. Hanicak, "Ice Gorges Terrorized."
166. "In Danger from Ice," *Baltimore Sun*, February 13, 1893.
167. Ibid.
168. High tides in Port Deposit are typically between one and three feet in height.
169. Ibid.
170. "ICE GORGES CAUSE FLOODS," *New York Times*.
171. *New York Times*, March 1, 1903.
172. Ibid.
173. Barry, *Susquehanna River Valley*, 126.
174. Hanicak, "Ice Gorges Terrorized."
175. *Cecil Democrat*, February 1847.
176. Ibid.
177. Ibid.
178. The Historical Society of Cecil County has a collection of images, which it has shared online (www.cecilhistory.org); Miller, *Cecil County*, 173.
179. Cecil County, "Ice and Water Overflowed."

NOTES TO PAGES 66–76

180. Ibid.
181. Miller, *Cecil County*, 173.
182. Healy, *Great Storms*, 94.
183. Pennsylvania Department of Environmental Protection, "The Flood of January 1996—A Special Hydrologic Report," www.dep.state.pa.us.
184. Ibid.
185. Ibid.
186. Sturgill, "Devastating History."
187. Ibid.
188. Ibid.

Chapter 10

189. Raphael, "Worst Winter Ever"; World History, "Revolutionary Soldiers."
190. "Letters of Jonathan Boucher," *Maryland Historical Magazine*, 232–41.
191. Ibid.
192. "Reminiscences," *Maryland Historical Magazine*.
193. Ibid.
194. Naval Historical Center Department of the Navy, "Naval War of 1812."
195. Ludlum, *American Winters I, 1604–1820*, 89–98; *Norfolk Gazette and Public Ledger*, February 1, 1815; Griffin, *Annals of Baltimore*, n.p.
196. A longboat is a large boat that may be launched from a sailing vessel. A jolly is a small boat that is usually hoisted at a ship's stern. The HMS *Dauntless* was a twenty-six-gun sloop. Stewart, "Battle of the Ice Mound."
197. Stewart, "Battle of the Ice Mound."
198. Ibid.
199. Ibid.
200. *Maryland Gazette* and *Political Intelligencer*, "Battle of the Ice Mound."
201. Ibid.
202. Ibid.
203. Stewart, "Battle of the Ice Mound."
204. Isacsson, "Surrat and the Lincoln Assassination."
205. Ibid.
206. Ibid.

Chapter 11

207. Brewington, "Chesapeake Bay Pilots."
208. Ibid.
209. Approximately four hundred islands that were charted on navigation charts in the late 1700s have disappeared.
210. De Gast, *Lighthouses*, 173.

211. Ibid.

212. Cronin, "Endangered Lighthouses."

213. Trapani, *Lighthouses of Maryland, Virginia*, 166.

214. De Gast, *Lighthouses*, 173.

215. Trapani, *Lighthouses of Maryland, Virginia*, 166; Healy, *Great Storms*, 68–70.

216. Fresnel lenses are lightweight but bend light as much as considerably thicker and heavier glass lenses.

217. Trapani, *Lighthouses of Maryland, Virginia*, 166; Healy, *Great Storms*, 68–70; Vojtect, *Lighting the Bay*, 194.

218. Healy, *Great Storms*, 68–70.

219. Trapani, *Lighthouses of Maryland, Virginia*, 166.

220. These are shaped like sparkplugs with lanterns on top, and they sit on concrete or metal caissons.

221. Ibid.

222. De Gast, *Lighthouses*, 173; Healy, *Great Storms*, 68–70.

223. Ibid.

224. Ibid.

225. Trapani, *Lighthouses of Maryland, Virginia*, 166.

226. No mention of an exact location is given. Trapani, *Lighthouses of Maryland, Virginia*, 166.

227. Trapani, *Lighthouses of Maryland, Virginia*, 166.

228. Ibid.

229. Ibid.

230. Healy, *Great Storms*, 68–70.

231. Krikstan, "Eleven Lighthouses"; Unicorn Book Shop, "History of Maryland Weather."

Chapter 12

232. Palmer, "Delmarva."

233. Chesapeake Bay Maritime Museum, "Oyster Wars," www.cbmm.org.

234. See chapter 17.

235. Maloney, "Chesapeake Odyssey."

236. Oysters for the Bay, "How It Used to Be," 2019, www.oystersforthebay.com.

237. Marden, "Sailing Oystermen."

238. "Oyster Season Opens on a Down Note," *Bay Journal*, 2017, www.bayjournal.com.

239. Marden, "Sailing Oystermen."

240. Kenney, "Chesapeake Country."

241. Ibid.

242. Palmer, "Delmarva."

243. Chesapeake Bay Maritime Museum, "Oyster Wars."

244. Ibid.

245. Ibid.

246. Maloney, "Chesapeake Odyssey."
247. Museum of American History, "Chesapeake Oysters," 2020, www.americanhistory.si.edu.
248. Mariners Museum, "Oyster Wars of the Lower Chesapeake Bay," www.marinersmuseum.org.
249. "Shot Down," *Democrat and News*.
250. Ibid.
251. Ibid.
252. Ibid.
253. Marden, "Sailing Oystermen."
254. Ibid.
255. MSX and Dermo are two parasites that have invaded the bay's oyster population. Starting around the late 1950s, these parasites spread to the extent that almost no oyster remains unaffected. Marden, "Sailing Oystermen."
256. Blackistone, *Dancing with the Tide*, 3–50.
257. Livie, *Chesapeake Oysters*, 73–93.
258. Palmer, "Delmarva."
259. Kenney, "Chesapeake Country"; De Gast, *Oysters*, 173.

Chapter 13

260. Nighttime temperatures can fall dramatically on clear nights when snow covers the ground, as snow is a very efficient emitter of longwave radiation.
261. *Maryland Weather Service, 1907*, 397–99.
262. Ibid.
263. Ibid.
264. *Newport News Daily Press*, March 1, 1904.
265. *Maryland Weather Service, 1907*, 397–99.
266. *Baltimore Sun*, January 24, 1977; *Baltimore Sun*, January 17, 1912.
267. Ibid.
268. "Coldest Day Recorded," *Baltimore Sun*, February 14, 1917.
269. Ibid.
270. Ibid.
271. Engelbrecht, "Severe Ice Conditions," 112–16.
272. LeGrand, "Big Chill."
273. *Newport News Daily Press*, January 2, 1918.
274. LeGrand, "Big Chill."
275. "Bay Boats Stopped: Big Ships Held Fast," *Baltimore Sun*, January 3, 1918.
276. "Warship Chaperones 10 Ships Down River," *Baltimore Sun*, January 14, 1918.
277. The U.S entered the Great War (World War I) in April 1917. This war ended on November 11, 1918.
278. "Warship Off in Huff," *Baltimore Sun*, January 24, 1918.
279. Ibid.

280. Ibid.
281. "Warship to Break Ice," *Baltimore Sun*, January 28, 1918.
282. "Warship Icebreaker Is Forced to Anchor," *Baltimore Sun*, January 28, 1918.
283. "Beached Steamer in Danger," *Baltimore Sun*, February 6, 1918.
284. "Ships on Schedule Despite Bay Ice," *Baltimore Sun*, February 12, 1918.
285. A note at the top of the *Sun's* January 14, 1918 edition alerted readers: "Tomorrow will be Meatless Day....If you want to beat the Germans, use no meat tomorrow. Fish and fowl do not count." "Trucks Bringing Oysters," *Baltimore Sun*, January 30, 1918.
286. "Trucks Bringing Oysters," *Baltimore Sun*, January 30, 1918.
287. Reno, "Cold Enough."
288. "Iceboat Out to Buck Gorges in the Bay," *Baltimore Sun*, January 26, 1920.
289. Ibid.
290. Matthews, "Ice on the World," 79–119.
291. Bentztown Bard, "Good Morning!" *Baltimore Sun*, January 26, 1948.

Chapter 14

292. Ludlum, *American Weather Book*, 298.
293. Bodine, *Chesapeake Bay*, 160.
294. "Six Firemen Hurt in Crash of Truck," *Baltimore Sun*, January 28, 1936.
295. LeGrand, "Big Chill."
296. "Six Firemen Hurt," *Baltimore Sun*.
297. Ibid.
298. Ibid.
299. Lewis, "Winter Weather"; Babcock, "40 Years Ago."
300. LeGrand, "Big Chill."
301. Ibid.
302. Harold G. Wheatley, "This Is My Island, Tangier," *National Geographic Magazine*, February 1973.
303. Jakon Hays, "Back in the Day: Frozen in Time. There Was No Motion in the Ocean Back in 1936," *Virginian-Pilot*, December 28, 2017.
304. *Baltimore Sun*, February 1936; *Baltimore Sun*, February 26, 1926.
305. Sandra Lee Anderson, "Snowed In," *Bay Weekly*, March 7–13, 2013.
306. LeGrand, "Big Chill."
307. "Cold Spell Longest Since 1936," *Baltimore Sun*, February 10, 1948.
308. "Unloading of Coal Cars Slowed by Cold Wave," *Baltimore Sun*, February 10, 1948.
309. "Breakers Fight 12-Foot Bay Ice," *Baltimore Sun*, February 10, 1948.
310. Bentztown Bard, "Good Morning!" *Baltimore Sun*, January 5, 1948.
311. Ibid., February 27, 1934.
312. Ibid., January 8, 1948.
313. Ibid., February 23, 1934; March 3, 1947; January 26, 1948; February 6, 1948; February 18, 1948.

314. William Sandler, "The Bentztown Bard" *Baltimore Sun*, May 18, 1987, www.baltimoresun.com.

315. "Wind and Icy Rain Sweep Over State," *Baltimore Sun*, January 10, 1956.

316. Ibid.; Anderson, "Snowed In."

317. Engelbrecht, "Severe Ice Conditions," 112–16.

318. Ibid.

319. Ibid.

320. Ibid.

321. Ibid.

322. Ibid.

323. Officially known as the William Preston Lane Jr. Memorial Bridge.

324. A second span opened in June 1973.

325. Roads to the Future, "Chesapeake Bay Bridge," www.roadstothefuture.com.

326. Engelbrecht, "Severe Ice Conditions," 112–16.

327. Ibid.

328. Chesapeake Bay Bridge-Tunnel, www.cbbt.com.

329. Ambrose and Weiss, *Washington Weather*, 252; Richmond, Virginia, recorded fifteen inches of snow; further inland, Big Meadows, Virginia, measured forty-two inches on March 6 and 7.

330. Forster, "Men Split the Sea."

331. "Piles of Ice in Upper Bay Snarl Ships," *Baltimore Sun*, January 2, 1963.

332. Ibid.

Chapter 15

333. U.S. Department of Commerce (NOAA/National Weather Service), "Temperature Departure"; Wagner, "Record-Breaking Winter," 65–69.

334. Known for generating storms, the Aleutian Low is a semipermanent area of low pressure positioned in the Gulf of Alaska, near the Aleutian Islands.

335. Wagner, "Circulation and Weather," 25–31.

336. U.S. Department of Commerce (NOAA), Metropolitan Climatological Summaries, National Capital Area: August 1976 and September 1976.

337. Now Thurgood Marshall International Airport.

338. Now Reagan Washington Airport.

339. U.S. Department of Commerce (NOAA), Metropolitan Climatological Summaries, National Capital Area: October 1976.

340. Ibid., November 1976.

341. Ibid., December 1976.

342. Ibid., January 1977.

343. As mapped from Landsat and NOAA satellite imagery.

344. U.S. Department of Commerce (NOAA), Metropolitan Climatological Summaries, National Capital Area: February 1977.

345. U.S. Coast Guard, U.S. Department of Transportation, Commander CG Group, Baltimore, Maryland, 1977.

346. Ibid.
347. Moyer, "Ice Conditions," 137–41; Foster, Schultz and Dallum, "Ice Conditions"; Foster, "Ice Observations."
348. Duffy, "Eastern Shore Deep Freeze."
349. Lewis, "Winter Weather."
350. Danny B., "Danny Bs Local History," www.facebook.com.
351. Duffy, "Eastern Shore Deep Freeze."
352. Selection of headlines, *Washington Post*, January 11–31, 1977.
353. Duffy, "Eastern Shore Deep Freeze."
354. Ibid.
355. Ibid.
356. Duffy, "Eastern Shore Deep Freeze."
357. Richard Polk, "Pair Walks Across River," *Baltimore Sun*, January 27, 1977.
358. Ibid.
359. *Washington Star*, January 1977.
360. Ibid.
361. Babcock, "40 Years Ago."
362. Wagner, "Record-Breaking Winter," 65–69.

Chapter 16

363. U.S. Department of Commerce (NOAA), Metropolitan Climatological Summaries, National Capital Area: December 1977, January 1978 and February 1978.
364. Ibid., November 1977.
365. Ibid., December 1977.
366. Wagner, "Record-Breaking Winter," 65–69.
367. U.S. Coast Guard, U.S. Department of Transportation, Commander CG Group, Baltimore, Maryland, 1978.
368. Foster, "Ice Observations."
369. Ibid., 1978.
370. Foster and Leffler, "Extreme Weather."
371. U.S. Department of Commerce (NOAA), Metropolitan Climatological Summaries, National Capital Area: October 1978, November 1978, December 1978, January 1979 and February 1979.
372. Foster and Leffler, "Extreme Weather."
373. Kocin and Uccellini, *Northeast Snowstorms*, 202–28.
374. Phil McCombs, "Part of Liquefied Natural Gas Pier Damaged by Ice in Chesapeake Bay," *Washington Post*, February 24, 1979.
375. U.S. Coast Guard, U.S. Department of Transportation, Commander CG Group, Baltimore, Maryland, 1979.
376. John Tierney, "Another Harsh Winter is Forecast: 4th Very Cold Spell in Row Seen for Area," *Washington Star*, December 9, 1979.

377. Ibid.
378. Ibid.
379. "Iceboats Sail Again," *Star Democrat*, January 28, 1970.
380. The first iceboats of this class were built during the winter of 1936–37.
381. Kelly L. Allen, "Cold a Boon for Ice Boaters," *Star Democrat*, January 23, 2009.
382. "55 Boats Qualify for Championship," *Baltimore Sun*, February 7, 1977.
383. Ibid.
384. Ibid.
385. Robert L. DuPont Jr., "Michigan Ice Boater Wins Title," *Baltimore Sun*, February 1977.
386. U.S. Department of Commerce (NOAA), Metropolitan Climatological Summaries, National Capital Area: December 1980, January 1981 and February 1981.
387. U.S. Coast Guard, U.S. Department of Transportation, Commander CG Group, Baltimore, Maryland, 1981.
388. Eileen Canzian, "Oysterman, Stranded on Icy Bay, Is Rescued Just in Time by Copter," *Baltimore Sun*, January 12, 1981.
389. Ibid.
390. Ibid.
391. See chapter 17 for more information on the ways of the watermen during this winter and other cold winters.
392. Dowgiallo, Predoehl and Stumpf, NOAA Technical Memorandum NESDIS AISC 14, Washington, D.C., June 1988.
393. Dale Russakoff, "Governor Seeks Aid for Icy Bay," *Washington Post*, January 1982.
394. Extremely cold air that plunges into North America from its source area in eastern Siberia.
395. David Michael Ettlin, "Arctic Winds Ice Roads, Dispelling Brief Warm Spell," *Baltimore Sun*, January 17, 1982.
396. History, "Plane Crashes into Potomac."
397. On December 8, 1963, a Pan Am aircraft, struck by lightning, crashed near the head of the Bay (outside of Elkton, Maryland), killing all eighty-one aboard.
398. History, "Plane Crashes into Potomac."
399. Ibid.
400. Ibid.
401. Frank D. Roylance, "Scorecard on the Winter of 93–94," *Baltimore Sun*, March 20, 1994.
402. U.S. Coast Guard, "Winter Freeze," 2–5.

Chapter 17

403. Wilson and Dize, personal conversation.
404. Ibid.
405. Kenney, "Chesapeake Country."
406. Marden, "Sailing Oystermen."

407. Palmer, "Delmarva."
408. Maloney, "Chesapeake Odyssey."
409. Blackistone, *Dancing with the Tide*, 45–50.
410. Ibid.
411. Quotes of Hal Borland, staff writer and editorialist for the *New York Times.*
412. "Life and Death on the Chesapeake," *Washington Post*, May 2, 1983.
413. Blackistone, *Dancing with the Tide*, 45–50.
414. V-shaped boats were easier to build than rounded-bottom boats.
415. Luis Marsden, "The Sailing Oystermen of Chesapeake Bay," *National Geographic Magazine*, December 1967.
416. Mariner's Museum, "Chesapeake Bay Workboats," 2020, www.marinersmuseum. org.

Chapter 18

417. Chris Guy, *Sun Papers*, January 30, 2000, B1.
418. Anderson, "Coast Guard Cutters."
419. "Tough Going on the Bay," *Star Democrat*, February 6, 2004
420. Lynn Anderson, "Ice as Far as You Can See," *Baltimore Sun*, February 3, 2004.
421. Ibid.
422. Bellprat, et al., "Role of Arctic Sea Ice."
423. Parker, "Icebreaker a Vital Lifeline."
424. Murray, "Icy Delaware Bay."
425. Bellprat, et al., "Role of Arctic Sea Ice."
426. Parker, "Icebreaker a Vital Lifeline."
427. Ibid.
428. Scott Dance, "Icebreakers Called Out to Clear Waterways," *Baltimore Sun*, January 9, 2018.
429. Virginia Marine Resources Commission, "Agency News," 2018, www.mrc. virginia.gov.
430. Susan San Felice, "Stuck with Nowhere to Go," *Washington Times*, January 16, 2018.
431. Ibid.
432. U.S. Coast Guard, U.S. Department of Transportation, Commander CG Group, Baltimore, Maryland, 1978.
433. United State Coast Guard, "Coast Guard Sets Seasonal Ice Condition 2 in Northern Chesapeake Bay and Tributaries," 2018, www.content.govdelivery.com.
434. Ibid.
435. Gamp, "Icebreaking Procedures," 210–16.
436. Ibid.
437. Robert Ruby, "Icebreaker's Job Is Ram, Crush, Shove," *Baltimore Sun*, January 21, 1982.
438. Ibid.
439. Ibid.

Epilogue

440. Canby, "Weather Went Wild," 798–829.
441. Unicorn Book Shop, "History of Maryland Weather."
442. Massachusetts Historical Society, "Samuel Sewall Diary."
443. Kupperman, "Seventeenth Century New England."
444. Hall, *Narratives, 1633–16*, 78.
445. The exact date of the greatest ice extent is not known with certainty for big ice years before 1750. The maximum ice extent in the winter of 1976–77 occurred in late January and early February.
446. See chapters 4 and 5.
447. NOAA, "Great Lakes Environmental Research: Historical Great Lakes Ice Cover," www.glerl.noaa.gov.
448. Borunda, "Great Lakes Ice Loss."
449. Isotherms are lines on a map that represent areas with the same temperature; Rutgers University Global Snow Lab, "Winter"; Lindsey, "Warming Winters."
450. Minimum temperatures for the winter of 2014–15 were much colder than normal (15° Fahrenheit colder in February at BWI) but are not shown in the chart on page 167.

Ice on the Chesapeake

451. Bentztown Bard, "Good Morning!" February 23, 1934.

Appendices

452. Strainers are filters that are designed to remove large contamination particles (over forty microns in diameter).

SELECTED BIBLIOGRAPHY

Ambrose, K., D. Henry and A. Weiss. *Washington Weather*. N.p.: Historical Enterprises, 2002.

Anderson, Lynn. "Coast Guard Cutters Clear Chesapeake Bay's Shipping Channels." *Star Democrat*, February 4, 2004.

Babcock, Jason. "40 Years Ago, Bay Froze Over." *Calvert Recorder*, February 8, 2017.

Barry, David A. *Maryland's Lower Susquehanna River Valley*. Charleston, SC: The History Press, 2009.

Bellprat, Omar, Javier García-Serrano, Neven S. Fuckar, François Massonnet, Virginie Guemas and Francisco J. Doblas-Reyes. "The Role of Arctic Sea Ice and Sea Surface Temperatures on the Cold 2015 February Over North America." *Bulletin of the American Meteorological Society* 97, no. 12 (December 2016): S36–S41.

Blackistone, Mick. *Dancing with the Tide: Watermen of the Chesapeake*. Centreville, MD: Tidewater Publishers, 2001.

Bodine, Aubrey A. *Chesapeake Bay and Tidewater*. New York: Bonanza Books, 1980.

Borunda, Alejandra. "Great Lakes Ice Loss: A Future Less Frozen." *National Geographic Magazine*, September 2020.

Boyd, Julian P., ed. "James Madison to Thomas Jefferson, Orange, Virginia, February 11, 1784." In *The Papers of Thomas Jefferson*. Princeton, NJ: Princeton University Press, 1952.

Brewington, M.V. "The Chesapeake Bay Pilots." *Maryland Historical Magazine*, June 1953, 122–24.

Canby, Thomas Y. "The Year the Weather Went Wild." *National Geographic Magazine*, December 1977, 798–829.

Clayton, John. "A Letter from Mr. John Clayton Rector of Crofton at Wakefield in Yorkshire, to the Royal Society, May 12, 1688. Giving an Account of

Several Observables in Virginia, and in His Voyage Thither, More Particularly Concerning the Air." *Philosophical Transactions of the Royal Society of London* 17 and 18 (1688): 17:781–95, 17:941–48, 18:121–35.

Cronin, William B. "The Chesapeake Bay's Endangered Lighthouses." *Maryland Magazine*, Summer 1990.

———. *Disappearing Islands of the Chesapeake Bay*. Johns Hopkins University Press, Baltimore, Maryland, 2005.

Davis, Neil. *Alaska Science Nuggets*. Fairbanks: Geophysical Institute of the University of Alaska, 1982.

De Gast, Robert. *Lighthouses of the Chesapeake Bay*. Baltimore, MD: Johns Hopkins University Press, 1973.

———. *Oysters of the Chesapeake*. First American Edition. New York: International Marine Publishing Company, 1970.

Democrat and News. "Shot Down on Deck." February 25, 1888.

"Deposition in the Land Records." *Maryland Historical Magazine*, March 1925, 383.

"The Diary of Egbert Gilmor." *Maryland Historical Magazine*, September 1922.

Dias, Henry, and Robert Quayle. "NOAA report." *NOAA, Environmental Data and Information* 11, no. 1 (January 1980).

Diggins, Milt. "Bridging Port Deposit 'Off from the World and the Rest of Mankind.'" *Maryland Historical Magazine*, Summer 2006, 185–202.

———. *Cecil County: Images of America*. Charleston, SC: Arcadia Publishing, 2008.

Dodds, Richard J. *Islands in a River: Solomons and Brooms Islands, Maryland*. Solomons, MD: Calvert Marine Museum, 2008.

Dorsey, Rhoda M. "The Conduct of Business in Baltimore, 1783–1785 as Seen in the Letterbook of Johnson, Johonnot and Co." *Maryland Historical Magazine*, Fall 1960, 230–42.

Dowgiallo, Michael J., Martin C. Predoehl and Richard P. Stumpf. NOAA Technical Memorandum NESDIS AISC 14. Washington, D.C., June 1988.

Earle, Swepson. "The Great Bay." In *Chesapeake Bay Country*. Baltimore, MD: Thomsen-Ellis Company, 1923.

Emerson, John C., Jr. "Book Review: *Steam Navigation in Virginia and North Carolina Waters, 1826–1836*." *Maryland Historical Magazine*, September 1950, 453.

Engelbrecht, Howard. "Severe Ice Conditions on Chesapeake Bay during the Winter of 1960–61." *Mariners Weather Log*, 1961, 112–16.

Fisher, Allan C., Jr. "My Chesapeake—Queen of Bays." *National Geographic Magazine*, 1980, 428–67.

Footner, Hulbert. *Rivers of the Eastern Shore: Seventeen Maryland Rivers*. Centreville, MD: Tidewater Publishers, 1944.

Foster, James, and Robert Leffler. "The Extreme Weather of February 1979 in the Baltimore-Washington Area." *National Weather Digest*, 1979.

Foster, James. L. "Ice Observations on the Chesapeake Bay 1977–1981." *Mariners Weather Log* 26, no 2 (1982): 65–71.

Foster, James L., Dorothy Schultz and William C. Dallum. "Ice Conditions on the Chesapeake Bay as Observed from Landsat During the Winter of 1977."

Proceedings of the 35th Eastern Snow Conference. White River Junction, New Hampshire, 1978.

Franklin, Benjamin. "Meteorological Imaginations and Conjectures." *Memoirs of the Literary and Philosophical Society of Manchester* 2 (December 1784): 357–61.

Gamp, Henry W. "Icebreaking Procedures on the Upper Chesapeake Bay." *Proceedings of the Marine Safety Council* 36 (December 1979): 210–16.

Gelber, Ben. *The Pennsylvania Weather Book*. New Brunswick, NJ: Rutgers University Press, 2002.

Griffin, Thomas W. *Annals of Baltimore*. Baltimore, MD: William Wooddy, 1821.

Hall, Clayton Colman, ed. *Narratives of Early Maryland, 1633–1684, A Character of the Province of Maryland by George Alsop: The Economy of Maryland in the 1660s*. New York: Charles Scribner's Sons, 1910.

Healy, David. *Great Storms of the Chesapeake*. Charleston, SC: The History Press, 2012.

Hess, Earl J. *A Study of Military Transportation*. Baton Rouge: Louisiana State University Press, 2017.

Hoffman, David. "Who's Killing the Chesapeake Bay?" *Washington Post Magazine*, April 1979.

Hoffman, Ronald. "The Carroll Family of Maryland." *Proceedings of the Maryland Antiquarian Society* 17, no. 2 (October 2007): 331–50. www.americanantiquarian.org.

Howard, Luke. *The Climate of London: Deduced from Meteorological Observations, Made in Different Places, in the Neighbourhood of the Metropolis*. 2 vols. Dublin, IE: SATTAL, 1820.

Isaacson, Alfred. "John Surrat and the Lincoln Assassination Plot." *Maryland Historical Magazine*, December 1957, 316–42.

Jefferson, Thomas. *Notes on the State of Virginia*. Boston: Lilly and Wait, 1781.

J.G.S. "Early Spanish Explorations and Adventures in Chesapeake Bay." *Historical Magazine*, 1859.

Kalm, Peter. *En Rasa til Norra America*. 3 vols. Sweden: John R. Forster, printed by William Eyres, 1753–61. Translated in 1771. Additional material published by Adolph E. Benson, ed. *Peter Kalm's Travels in North America*. New York, Wilson-Erickson Inc., 1937.

Kenney, Nathaniel T. "Chesapeake Country." *National Geographic Magazine*, September 1964.

Kocin, Paul J., and Louis W. Uccellini. *Northeast Snowstorms, Volume 1: Overview*. Boston: American Meteorological Society, 2004.

———. *Snowstorms Along the Northeast Coast of the United States: 1955 to 1985*. Boston: American Meteorological Society, 1990.

Lambert, John Ralph, Jr., ed. "Travels of an English Immigrant to Maryland in 1796–97." *Maryland Historical Magazine*, June 1918, 81–95.

LeGrand, Marty. "The Big Chill." *Chesapeake Bay Magazine*, February 2004.

"Letters of Jonathan Boucher." *Maryland Historical Magazine*, September 1914, 232–41. (The letters and memoranda are all dated from January and February 1780.)

Levin, Alexander Lee. "How Commodore Joshua Barney Outwitted the British at Norfolk." *Maryland Historical Magazine*, Summer 1978, 163–67.

Livie, Kate. *Chesapeake Oysters*. Charleston, SC: The History Press, 2015.

Ludlum, David M. *The American Weather Book*. Boston: Houghton Mifflin Company, 1982.

———. *Early American Winters I, 1604–1820*. Boston: American Meteorological Society, 1966.

———. *Early American Winters II, 1821–1870*. Boston: American Meteorological Society, 1968.

———. "The Famous Susquehanna Ice Bridge of 1852." *Weatherwise*, December 1954.

Marden, Luis. "The Sailing Oystermen of the Chesapeake Bay." *National Geographic Magazine*, December 1967.

Maryland Gazette and *Political Intelligencer*. "Battle of the Ice Mound Dated from Easton Feb. 19, An Account by Joseph Stewart's Account." February 23, 1815.

Maryland Weather Service, 1899. Vol. 1. Baltimore, MD: J.H. Press, 1899.

Maryland Weather Service, 1907. Vol. 2. Baltimore, MD: J.H. Press, 1907.

Matthews, Samuel W. "Ice on the World." *National Geographic Magazine*, January 1987, 79–119.

McGrath, Peter, and Mary Hager. "An American Treasure at Risk." *Newsweek Magazine*, December 1983.

Mechanics' Magazine and Journal of Science, Arts and Manufacturers 56 (1852): 455–56.

Middleton, Arthur P. *Tobacco Coast*. Newport News, VA: Mariners Museum, 1953.

Miers, Earl Schenk. *The Drowned River: The Real Story of the Chesapeake Bay*. Newark, DE: Curtis Paper Company, 1967.

Miller, Alice E. *Cecil County, Maryland: A Study in Local History*. Elkton, MD: C&L Printing and Specialty Company, 1949.

Moody, Robert E. "Thomas Gorges, Proprietary Governor of Maine, 1640–1643." In *Proceedings of the Massachusetts Historical Society*. Third series. Vol. 75. N.p.: n.p., 1963.

Morgan, Michael. *Deadly Storms of the Delmarva Coast*. Charleston, SC: The History Press, 2019.

Moyer, Joseph. "Chesapeake Bay Ice Conditions, 1976–77." *Mariners Weather Log*, 1977, 137–41.

Niles, H., ed. *Niles Weekly Register*, 1838.

Norfolk Gazette and Public Ledger. February 1, 1815.

Palmer, Catherine Bell. "'Delmarva' Gift of the Sea." *National Geographic Magazine*, September 1950.

Pierre, Catherine. "Treasured Islands." *Johns Hopkins Magazine*, November 2005.

"Reminiscences of Thomas Ridout." *Maryland Historical Magazine*, September 1925, 215–35.

Reno, L. "Cold Enough Yet." *Calvert Gazette*, January 3, 2013.

Rossignol, Ken. *Chesapeake 1850*. N.p.: Privateer Clause Publishing, 2012.

Ruffin, Edmund. "The Diary of Edmund Ruffin of Prince George County." *William and Mary Quarterly* (Williamsburg), April 1915, 247.

Scharf, Thomas J. *The Chronicles of Baltimore*. Baltimore, MD: Turnbull Bros., 1874.

Shomette, Donald G. *Shipwrecks on the Chesapeake, 1608–1978.* Centreville, MD: Tidewater Publishers, 1982.

Skaggs, David C., and Richard K. Macmaster, eds. "Post-Revolutionary Letters of Alexander Hamilton, Piscataway Merchant (Part 1), January–June 1784." *Maryland Historical Magazine*, December 1968.

Sommerville, Charles William. "Early Career of Governor Francis Nicholson." *Maryland Historical Magazine*, June 1909, 101–14.

Stewart, Robert G. "The Battle of the Ice Mound, February 7, 1815." *Maryland Historical Magazine*, Winter 1975, 372–78.

Trapani, Bob, Jr. *Lighthouses of Maryland, Virginia: History, Mystery, Legends and Lore.* N.p.: Myst and Lace Publishers Inc., 2006.

U.S. Coast Guard. "Winter Freeze Blankets East: Cities Warm, Ships Moving Thanks to Coast Guard Crews." *Commandant's Bulletin*, April 1994, 2–5.

U.S. Coast Guard and U.S. Department of Transportation. Commander CG Group, Baltimore, Maryland, 1977–79.

U.S. Department of Commerce (NOAA). Metropolitan Climatological Summaries, National Capital Area: October 1976–February 1977.

———. Metropolitan Climatological Summaries, National Capital Area: October 1977–February 1978.

———. Metropolitan Climatological Summaries, National Capital Area: October 1978–February 1979.

U.S. Department of Commerce (NOAA/National Weather Service). "Depth of Snow on the Ground: January 31, 1977." *Weekly Weather and Crop Bulletin*, 1977.

———. "Temperature Departure from 30-Year Mean: January 1977." *Weekly Weather and Crop Bulletin*, 1977.

Vojtect, Pat. *Lighting the Bay: Tales of Chesapeake Lighthouses.* Centreville, MD: Tidewater Publishers, 1996.

Wagner, James. "The Circulation and Weather of 1977." *Weatherwise* 31, no. 1 (1978): 25–31.

———. "The Record-Breaking Winter of 1976–77." *Weatherwise* 30, no. 2 (1977): 65–69.

Warden, David Bailie. "Journal of a Voyage from Annapolis to Cherbourg on Board the Frigate *Constitution*, 1 August to 6 September 1811." *Maryland Historical Magazine*, June 1916, 127–42.

Webster, Noah. *A Collection of Papers on Political, Literary and Moral Subjects.* New York: Webster and Clark, 1843.

Wilson, Robbie, and Russel Dize. Personal conversation, 2018.

Wilson, W.B. *History of the Pennsylvania Railroad.* Philadelphia, PA: n.p., 1889.

Wood, Gillen D'Arcy. *Tambora: The Eruption That Changed the World.* Princeton, NJ: Princeton University Press, 2015.

Primary Newspapers Sources

Annapolis Gazette (Annapolis, MD)
Baltimore Sun (Baltimore, MD)
Cecil Democrat (Elkton, MD)
Cecil Whig (Elkton, MD)
Centreville Times (Centreville, MD)
Daily Times (Salisbury, MD)
Havre de Grace Republican (Havre de Grace, MD)
Maryland Gazette (Annapolis, MD)
Newport News Daily Press (Norfolk, VA)
New York Times (New York City)
Niles Weekly Register (Baltimore, MD)
Star Democrat (Easton, MD)
Virginia Gazette (Williamsburg, VA)
Virginia Journal and Alexandria Advertiser (Alexandria, VA)
Virginia Pilot (Norfolk, VA)
Washington Star (Washington, D.C.)

Internet Sources

American Naval Records Society. "Northern Lakes, and Pacific Ocean, Part 3 of 7, Bolton Landing, New York." www.ibiblio.org.
AmericanWX. "Mid-Atlantic Ice Analysis, February 20, 2015, MODIS image." www.americanwx.com.
Bay Trippers: An Online Field Trip to the Chesapeake Bay. www.baytrippers.thinkport.org.
"A Brief History of the Chesapeake and Delaware Canal." *Chesapeake Bay Magazine*, 2018. www.chesapeakebaymagazine.com.
Cecil County. "When Ice and Water Overflowed the Susquehanna River, the Media Descended on Port Deposit." www.cecilcounty.wordpress.com.
———. "When Ice Jammed the Susquehanna River and Threatened Port Deposit, Photographers Were Quick to Respond." www.cecilcounty.wordpress.com.
Chesapeake Bay Foundation. "More Than Just a Bay." www.cbf.org.
Chesapeake Bay Program. "Captain John Smith." www.chesapeakebay.net.
———. "Chesapeake Bay Geography." www.chesapeakebay.net.
"Coast Guard Cutter *Cleat* Breaking Ice in Maryland." February 23, 2015. www.youtube.com.
Daily Press. "Hampton Roads Deep Freeze of 1904, 1919, 1940 and 1958." www.dailypress.com.
Danny B's Local History and Other Kool Stuff. www.facebook.com.
Duffy, Jim. "The Great Eastern Shore Deep Freeze During the Winter of 1976–77." Secrets of the Eastern Shore. www.secretsoftheeasternshore.com.

Fishing Vermont. "How Ice Forms." www.fishingvermont.net.

Forster, Dave. "When Men Split the Sea: Building the Chesapeake Bridge-Tunnel." *Virginian-Pilot*, April 13, 2014. www.pilotonline.com.

"Frozen Chesapeake Bay 2015." February 24, 2015. www.youtube.com.

"Frozen Chesapeake Bay 2018." January 8, 2018. www.youtube.com.

Hall, Clayton Colman, ed. *Narratives of Early Maryland, 1633–1684: A Character of the Province of Maryland by George Alsop*. New York: Charles Scribner's Sons. www.archive.org.

Hanicak, Joan B. "When Ice Gorges Terrorized Port Deposit and the Susquehanna." *Delmarva History*, Sunday, January 24, 2016. www.facebook.com.

Historical Society of Cecil County. "Abraham Collection." www.teachers.ccps.org.

History. "This Day in History: Plane Crashes into Potomac." November 13, 2009. www.history.com.

Krikstan, Catherine. "Eleven Lighthouses in the Chesapeake Bay Watershed." www.chesapeakebay.net.

Lewis, Brent. "Winter Weather on the Chesapeake Bay." www.easternshorebrent.com.

Lindsey, Rebecca. "Warming Winters Across the United States." NOAA. www.climate.gov.

Maryland State Climatologist. "Monthly and Seasonal Climate Information." www.atmos.umd.edu.

Massachusetts Society Historical Papers. The Winthrop Papers Digital Edition, Papers of the Winthrop, Vol. 4. www.masshist.org.

Mechanics Magazine, Museum, Journal, Register, and Gazette 56. www.books.google.com.

Murray, Molly. "Icy Delaware Bay Draws a Crowd." *News Journal,* March 5, 2015. www.delmarvanow.com.

National Park Service. "John Smith's Journals." www.nps.gov.

Naval Historical Center Department of the Navy. "'The Naval War of 1812,' A Documentary History: Volume III 1814–1815, Chesapeake Bay." 2002. www.ibiblio.org.

New York Times. "ICE GORGES CAUSE FLOODS; Portions of Port Deposit, Md., and Meadville, Penn., Under Water." February 3, 1903. www.query.nytimes.com.

NOAA. "Mid-Atlantic Ice Analysis." February 20, 2015. www.natice.noaa.gov.

Parker, Susan. "Icebreaker a Vital Lifeline for Frozen Smith Island." *Delmarva Now*, January 9, 2018. www.13newsnow.com.

Pennsylvania DEP. "The Flood of January 1996—A Special Hydrologic Report." www.dep.state.pa.us.

Raphael, Ray. "America's Worst Winter Ever." *American History Magazine*, February 2010. www.historynet.com.

Rutgers University Global Snow Lab. "Spring North American Snow Extent." www.climate.rutgers.edu.

———. "Winter North American Snow Extent." www.climate.rutgers.edu.

Sturgill, Erika Quesenbery. "Port Deposit's Devastating History with Massive Ice Jams, Floods." *Cecil Whig,* January 18, 2014. www.cecildaily.com.

Swift, Earl. "The Incredible True Story of the *Henrietta C.*" *Outside*, 2018. www.outsideonline.com.

Unicorn Book Shop. "The History of Maryland Weather." www.unicornbookshop.com.

University of Maryland Center of Environmental Science. "Horn Point Oyster Hatchery." www.hatchery.hpl.umces.edu.

USGS. "1971: Largest Rivers of the U.S." www.pubs.usgs.gov.

Virginia Places. "Oysters in Virginia." www.virginiaplaces.org.

World History. "Revolutionary Soldiers in the Hard Winter of 1779–1780." June 22, 2017.www.worldhistory.us.

INDEX